Detecting Child Abuse
Recognizing Children at Risk through Drawings

Detecting Child Abuse

Recognizing Children at Risk
Through Drawings

LYNNE CANTLAY, PH.D.

HOLLY
PRESS
SANTA BARBARA, CA

Printed in the United States of America

Library of Congress Catalog Card Number 96-76093
Cantlay, Lynne
    Detecting child abuse: recognizing children at risk through drawings
    Includes bibliographies and index
    First Edition
    ISBN 0-9651068-2-9

Editor: Cheryl Crabtree
Book Design: Bill Horton
Publication Coordinator: Laura Davison

To Cameron, Corinna, Talia,
and all the children in the world.
May you all be safe.

Author and Publisher Disclaimer

This handbook is:

This handbook provides information to people who care for children: parents, day-care professionals, teachers, recreational guides, nannies, and others who have little or no knowledge of art therapy. It is designed to help laypersons recognize common signs of distress in children's drawings. The knowledge can help viewers determine whether to recommend professional evaluation by a child abuse expert.

The information herein is a compilation of indicators that commonly appear in the drawings of abused children. The information is not new—these indicators are found in numerous art therapy books authored by renowned researchers. This handbook simply presents information in a single, easy-to-use source. The information relates specifically to children's drawings and should not be generalized to all drawings.

This handbook is NOT a training manual:

This guide does not contain complete information regarding art therapy. It will not make readers experts in art therapy or child abuse. It should be used only as a general guide to help the reader take the first step in the decision to get professional help for a child at risk. It is NOT a final source in determining trauma—only a child abuse expert can properly assess and evaluate a child at possible risk.

Warning

When analyzing drawings, viewers must remember to shield their concern from the child. A child at possible risk must not be interrogated. Interrogation contaminates the situation and makes professional evaluation more difficult.

The publisher and author shall have neither liability nor responsibility to any person or entity with respect to the misuse of the information contained in this book. Every effort has been made to make this guide as accurate as possible. However, it may contain errors, both typographical and in content.

If you do not wish to be bound by the above, you may return this book to the publisher for a full refund.

C O N T E N T S

The idea for this handbook emerged a year ago during lunch with a friend, a first-year teacher. While talking about her class of second graders and their drawings, she began to frown. She started asking questions about a particular student's drawing. It looked "strange" to her but she didn't know why. "What does it mean when the eyes don't have any pupils?" she wondered. "Why is his self-portrait all in pieces?"

In response, I told my friend about a logical and consistent method of examining pictures. I explained that a viewer can find clues about the artist's internal state by analyzing drawings. My friend's frown turned to excitement. She said that if she could learn to recognize the clues or signs of distress in drawings, she could help troubled children receive expert counseling before problems became serious or intractable.

But my friend, a busy teacher, had no interest in studying art therapy in depth. She just wanted to be able to recognize stress or trauma in a drawing. She wanted to be alert to any child who might benefit from professional counseling.

After lunch, I mulled over the idea of compiling basic art therapy information from a multitude of sources into one handbook. The task seemed overwhelming. Many excellent single-volume books covering the subject already existed. However, all were standard book length. I then thought about devising an outline—a bare-bones skeleton—of certain characteristics in children's drawings that could help a layperson understand what makes a drawing seem "not right." (Characteristics are elements or parts of a drawing—body parts, different aspects of an object, different perspectives of drawing style and composition.)

I also thought about my own method of analyzing children's art, which developed from the numerous assessments that courts and attorneys have asked me to make during the past twenty years. Whenever I evaluate a drawing, I refer to many excellent art therapy sources. But the information is scattered throughout the books, and it takes time to find all the details I need. I recognized the value of having easy access to the basic information in a single source, along with a bibliography of original sources for readers who desire more detailed explanations.

My thoughts evolved into this guide: *Detecting Child Abuse: Recognizing Children at Risk through Drawings.* Designed for caregivers (parents, teachers, day care professionals) in the childcare arena, it provides basic tools for recognizing signs of distress in children's drawings. This recognition is important, since children rarely express disturbing feelings verbally. They are also too young to know that neglect, alcoholism, emotional abuse, and sexual abuse are unhealthy behaviors. Rather than verbalizing distress, children often express confusion and feelings through behaviors and drawings.

A caregiver who can recognize potential problems in artwork can be a great asset in childhood trauma prevention. Caregivers who work with many children the same age can easily recognize a picture that veers from the developmental norm. Children's drawings, despite unique creativity, are more alike than different in certain developmental traits and ability. While some children at risk provide more obvious clues of severe abuse in their drawings, most troubled children camouflage the content. But an alert caregiver will notice that something may be wrong from the way certain characteristics appear. She can then recommend a professional evaluation of the situation promptly, before the situation worsens.

Teachers and parents, the largest group of caregivers, will find this an especially useful guide. Childhood trauma is an emotional issue, and parents and teachers can easily jump to conclusions based on little information or just a sense that "something is wrong." The concrete characteristics and interpretations in this book, identified through years of research, will help readers be more objective when analyzing children's art.

For the sake of reading ease, I have used the feminine personal pronoun, rather than the cumbersome s/he and her/his, to represent the child and the reader. I have also used fictitious names in all examples, and any similarity to any situation the reader may find familiar is purely coincidental.

I hope you will find this handbook helpful and easy to use. The information is not new and many of you already know and recognize the characteristics I present. But finding all the basic information in a convenient single source will save you valuable time when you analyze drawings. I also hope that the systematic approach, based on extensive research by renowned art therapists, will help you be more objective. Most of all, I hope this guide will help us recognize—and act upon—the distress signals that children send through their art.

ACKNOWLEDGMENTS

I would like to thank all the art therapists who have spent their lives researching and substantiating the interpretations of characteristics found in this handbook. Without their work, children's drawings would still be ignored as a valuable source of information.

I feel honored to have so many wonderful people to thank. I am especially indebted to Alice Esbenshade and Samm Hawley who gave unflagging encouragement, support, and gentle prodding. They were early readers who shared many good ideas to make the handbook easier to use. My special thanks to Bob Klein for his suggestion to include a Reader's Workbook section and his patience and loving support.

I am indebted to Lucy Thomas who found important research articles that were impossible for me to locate. My profound appreciation to Beth Bornstein, Judith Brown, Shandra Campbell, Laura Davison, Violet Oaklander, Kim Omori, and Lucia Tebbe who read the manuscript and made valuable suggestions.

Special thanks go to Marlene Alarcon, Shandra Campbell, Cheryl Crabtree, Laura Davison, Anna Hayes, Kristen Kinsella, Dennis Naiman, Bronte Reynolds, Marlénè Roberts, Jeri Waite, and Jan Vucinich, who helped locate the drawings for the Developmental chapter.

Font expert and designer, Bill Horton, a genius in scanning and reproducing drawings whose details were hard to capture, also deserves special thanks. We will all appreciate the drawings he placed on top of each answer section in the Workbook everytime we use it.

There are no words to express my gratitude and love to the three people who made this book a true work of art. The book itself became a reality with Cheryl Crabtree, copy editor extraordinaire. Her editing is an art which leaves me with great awe and admiration. Laura Davison's vision, clarity, and production design skill made this book unique. Her careful handling and anticipation of all the details was and still is mind-boggling. I see her as the "General Contractor" and the house she built was more than I dreamed. Glenn Johnson, a brilliant artist and designer, created the perfect, "show-stopper" cover. Each of them caught the true essence of the book and brought my fantasy to life. My deepest thanks to each of them for the special attention they devoted to this book.

Best of all, this project became a work of love. The care and love that surrounded us while we agonized over selections, words, titles, fonts, colors, and size, the good humor and creative zest became infectious. My life felt blessed. With each new addition to the team the love grew exponentially. To all, my thanks and gratitude.

Lynne Cantlay
Santa Barbara, California

> Child abuse: *The physical or mental injury, sexual abuse, negligent treatment, or maltreatment of a child under the age of eighteen by a person who is responsible for the child's welfare under circumstances which indicate that the child's health or welfare is harmed or threatened.*
> (NATIONAL CENTER ON CHILD ABUSE AND NEGLECT. PUBLIC LAW 93-237)
>
> Child abuse: *Maltreatment with intentional harm or a threat to harm by anyone who is in the role of caregiver.*
> (WISSOW, 1995)

Child abuse has existed throughout recorded history.[1] In this century, healthy children—our most precious and valuable assets—have become increasingly vulnerable. Reports show that more and more children are suffering from trauma, often resulting in pathology.[2] In this handbook, children who might be in abusive situations as described above are "children at risk."

Fortunately, we are now more aware of the prevalence of child abuse. During the past decade, additional protective and legal agencies have been established to handle this phenomenon. We now also know how important it is to recognize children at risk at an early stage before the damage is too great. Caregivers play an important role in the recognition process. Any person who works or spends time with children should learn to recognize the warning signals of child abuse.

In an article on child abuse in *The New England Journal of Medicine*, Dr. L. S. Wissow defines four different kinds of child abuse:

Neglect
Failing to provide basic shelter, supervision, medical care, or support. This is thought to be the most common and probably most life-threatening type of abuse.

Physical Abuse
Inflicting bodily injury through excessive force. This also includes forcing a child to engage in physically harmful activity, such as excessive exercise.

Emotional Abuse
Controlling a child through coercion, physical and emotional withdrawal, love deprivation, and demeaning language and behavior.

Sexual Abuse
1) *Actual sexual contact between children and older people.*
2) *Using a child as an object, either passively or actively.*
3) *Using a child as a sexual stimulus for the adult.*
4) *Inappropriate exposure of a child or children to sexual acts or materials.*

---

[1] (DeMause, 1990, 1991)
[2] Any deviation from a healthy, normal, or efficient condition (*Webster's Unabridged Dictionary*)

1

Family Structure and Change

In the past several decades, the dynamics of the family system have changed dramatically. Economic conditions have forced both parents in most intact families[3] to produce income to survive. Hired caregivers are now a necessity for many families with two working parents. Children no longer remain in a familiar environment with an extended family and/or with a neighborhood mother. Instead, they are often shuttled from one caregiver to another. Consequently, they have become more accessible to relative strangers.

This is even more true in the case of single and divorced parents. Most must rely on professional caregivers to care for their children. As in typical intact families, most single parents live away from their families of origin and do not have extended families to help with childcare. Work hours are long and arduous. Their economic survival requires entrusting the care of their children to other people and/or day-care centers.

Early Recognition

Recognizing the symptoms of children at risk has become a critical task for all of us who work with children in a caretaking, healing, or educational role. We must be alert to the signs sent by children at risk, especially when these signs are disguised and communicated unconsciously. Children at risk have often been admonished "not to tell" and feel they need to repress the information or memory to survive. To ensure the safety of these children, we must judiciously and prudently examine the signs that are available to us as soon as possible.

Why Drawings?

Detecting Child Abuse: Recognizing Children at Risk through Drawings is a simple guide designed to help laypersons identify a troubled child—a possible victim of abuse or trauma—through drawings. Since most children draw for fun and all children draw in schools, drawings provide us with an abundant source of information that is readily available for observation and review. The guide points out characteristics in drawings that may indicate problems. This information can help laypersons identify obvious problem areas with consistency and accuracy and make an intelligent determination about a drawing. Finally, this guide is meant to encourage and instill enough confidence in caregivers to recommend outside evaluations of children at potential risk when necessary.

Research History

A set of three main categories and their characteristics form the core of this handbook: *person, house,* and *tree*. These are the most commonly drawn subjects in children's art, based on the research of numerous psychologists and art therapists who analyzed tens of thousands of children's drawings, over a period of forty years.

Most research in the art therapy field has been based on three techniques: The House-Tree-Person Technique (Buck, 1948), The Human Figure Drawing Test (Koppitz, 1968), and Kinetic Family Drawings (Burns, 1970). Drawings from these test techniques were used to create a baseline for evaluating and assessing children. After examining thousands of drawings, the researchers were able to develop the standards that are currently in use.

The relevant characteristics in this guide come from the sources listed in the bibliography. The references show consistent agreement regarding the

---

[3] family with mother, father, and children in the same home

listed characteristics. This consistency among the similarities of interpretation of the characteristics provides the reader with a common base. Many of the characteristics that indicate negative traits, problems, or abuse have emerged from longitudinal studies (over ten years) of drawings by abused children in shelter settings and from corresponding research studies that showed the significance of these traits.

Format

This handbook outlines a standardized procedure for identifying characteristics in a drawing that give cause for concern. The procedure will help you look at drawings to determine whether enough signs are present to warrant a more extensive evaluation. It presents the basic steps of drawing analysis, divided into three sections.

1. "Developmental Aspects of Drawing" shows the progression of abilities at each age level with examples of drawings.

2. The "Analyzing Drawings" chapter attempts to systematize an examination approach. This section will help you recognize and understand all aspects of the process.

3. The "Characteristics" chapter forms the heart of the handbook. It lists, in alphabetical order, the basic characteristics and their interpretations within the main subject categories: Person, House, and Tree, and additional sections on General Characteristics, Sexual Characteristics, and Frequently Drawn Miscellaneous Details.

Caveat

Emphasized throughout the handbook is a very important rule of thumb: *Always remember that you must look at all extenuating circumstances, behavior, personal history, and the developmental level of the child when analyzing a drawing.*

Another warning reappears in every chapter: *A pattern must be established in a number of drawings over a period of time.* You might then ask, How many drawings are sufficient? How much time is necessary before you feel you have gathered sufficient information to recommend professional evaluation? This is a judgment call that you must make. I can generalize by saying that in most normal cases the following timeline has worked for me:

If you see the child frequently (e.g., three or more times a week), you may have seen many drawings, but the time frame may be too short (e.g., one week). If the child is going through a transition or her environment or situation is in turmoil, it is prudent to wait until the situation has settled. If her drawings continue to show disturbing characteristics for nearly a month, the child needs help and it is wise to recommend evaluation.

If you see the child once a week, it will take at least a month to six weeks to determine whether her drawings are consistently disturbed. Many upsetting things can happen in a day and will appear in her drawings. Time will therefore determine whether a consistent pattern of disturbed drawings exists, or the child was merely expressing the disturbances of a particular day.

You may encounter other situations when very few drawings (six to eight) in a short period of time (say one week or two visits) are enough to request an evaluation. Other extenuating circumstances and evidence will corroborate your analysis—what the child reports, bruises, signs of neglect (e.g., no lunches, uncombed hair), and bizarre behavior. Your common sense will let you know when enough is enough.

Detecting Child Abuse is not a training manual. It is not meant to replace any of the excellent resource books written by experts in this field. Nor does this handbook provide the important background, theory, and justification of art therapy. Anyone interested in studying or understanding art therapy further should refer to the source material for detailed explanations (see Appendix and Bibliography).

Nor does this handbook in any way eliminate the need for a trained art therapist or psychologist to evaluate a child to determine whether she is truly at risk and needs professional help. A layperson will not become an expert after reading this book. *Detecting Child Abuse* is rather like a map. We can all read a map, but that ability does not make us cartographers.

DEVELOPMENTAL ASPECTS OF DRAWINGS

When you learn to recognize developmentally inappropriate drawings, you become sensitive to behavioral and other signs of distress much sooner. You can then consult with the family at an earlier stage and recommend professional assessment before the behavior becomes destructive. This chapter presents information about developmental levels and what might be considered appropriate and inappropriate drawing for a child's age.

Discrepancies

A critical warning flag in drawings is the difference between the developmental age level of the drawing and the actual age of the artist. Children normally draw according to their chronological age. If a difference appears, it is important to be watchful. *An obvious discrepancy between a child's age and the level of her drawings must be scrutinized.*

Important factors contributing to discrepancies are listed below and are discussed in this chapter:

1) A shift from age-appropriate drawing to a younger developmental level.
2) A change from well-organized figures to disorganized, incomplete bodies.
3) A change from appropriate representations to transparencies and unrealistic representations.
4) A change from complete representations to a lack of essential features in a house and/or tree.
5) A change from representational pictures to very primitive drawings.
6) The need for viewers to request clarification of a drawing when clarification was unnecessary in the past.

These changes indicate a problem. The reasons for discrepancies must be acknowledged when analyzing a drawing. The discrepancies could result from difficulties stemming from physiological problems, psychological issues, environmental situations, or combinations of the above. It is therefore important to evaluate the child and determine the nature of the problem.

Discrepancies do not always mean trauma, but they do indicate that something is amiss and merits observation. Nor are all discrepancies alarming. Common sense will tell you that a twelve-year-old child who draws like a five-year-old may be having problems, but a three-year-old who draws like a four-year-old is developmentally advanced.

The following case studies show different behaviors that coexist with discrepancies in drawings. These discrepancies and behavior patterns eventually brought the latent problems to light.

CASE STUDY 1

Tom, a bright, attractive seven-year-old, began "acting out" in class. Normally a very shy child, he became impulsive and was unable to control his outbursts. He was restless and expressed his hostility by pushing his classmates and calling them names. The situation finally reached a point where the teacher and principal were considering expelling Tom from school.

Tom's drawings were very primitive. He drew pictures of himself and his family by drawing only heads. Other objects he drew were not easily identifiable. His drawings were typical of a three-year-old child. In a meeting with his parents we explored what was happening in the family when he was three. The parents remembered that Tom was hospitalized for corrective eye surgery for three weeks. The forced separation during the hospital stay was traumatic for Tom, and he came home with night terrors.

Talking with the parents, I discovered that they were planning a month-long trip to Europe. This was restimulating Tom's fear of abandonment—the same fear he experienced when he was three. When we addressed this issue in therapy he relaxed. His acting out behavior stopped and his drawings reflected his age level. His last drawing was well organized and all the figures had bodies. The miscellaneous details were easily recognizable.

CASE STUDY 2

Annie, a very precocious seven-year-old, began "acting out" and making lewd sexual remarks in class. Her drawings shifted from well–organized figures to disorganized, incomplete drawings. Transparencies (X-ray-like abilities) appeared in all her drawings and many objects were unrecognizable.

Consultation with her parents disclosed that when Annie was four, her day care school was closed due to the discovery of sexual molestation in the school. The parents believed that Annie had escaped molestation because she reported that nothing had happened to her. It became clear in therapy that she indeed had been molested. She expressed her feelings of anger and confusion through her aggressive and sexually precocious behavior. After several

months of therapy, Annie was drawing at her age level and returned to normal behavior in the classroom.

CASE STUDY 3

David, age nine, had become very moody and extremely passive. His teacher reported he was a "sweet kid" and although he was not "acting out," it was apparent he had changed. He refused to talk about his feelings and was withdrawn. He stopped participating in class and playing with his classmates. He began drawing at the five-year-old level. Drawings of himself were elementary and his representations of his environment were unrealistic.

David's parents divorced when he was five. Four years later, he still had not accepted his parents' divorce. His father had recently remarried, but David continued to talk about "When mom and dad get together again...,"etc.

The stimulus for David's depression was his inability to accept his father's remarriage. In therapy David was finally able to express his feelings about the divorce and the remarriage. He learned to accept and express his anger and sadness. His depression lifted and he resumed his regular activities.

Developmental Levels in Years

Developmental levels are identified by age. As in all established patterns, children will follow their own schedule of development. However, most children will fit into a normal range. It is important to be aware that a drawing should be developmentally age appropriate. *(Kellogg, 1970; Klepsch and Logie, 1982)*

This brief developmental outline gives a basic idea of a child's normal capability at each age level. An understanding of age appropriateness is essential to determining regression, either intellectual or emotional. If a child regresses to a younger age level of drawing because of stress or trauma in her life, the drawings generally return to the appropriate age level when the stress is eliminated.

The following developmental levels are presented in a simplified format. Many caregivers and teachers care for groups of children approximately the same age. A simple way of detecting a regressed drawing is to compare it with the level of other drawings by children the same age.

For a more detailed explanation with many examples of children's drawings at each age level, Rhoda Kellogg's *Analyzing Children's Art* is an excellent resource.

Developmental Levels in Years

18 months to 2 ½ years

The drawings are mostly lines and scribbles. These non–goal-directed markings are used primarily for motor expression. A scribble begins with the dot and then moves to single lines, such as vertical, horizontal, diagonal, and curved, followed by multiples of these, and then to curving lines and loops, eventually culminating in a circle.

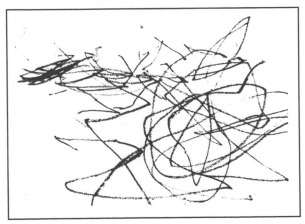

3 years

The three-year-old begins to outline form within the scribbles on a random basis. Gradually these shapes become familiar circles and squares of all sizes. What she calls people will be mostly circles with aggregates of circles and squares and lines for facial features. She may begin with a plan but will not know what she is drawing until it is done and can then tell a story about her drawing.

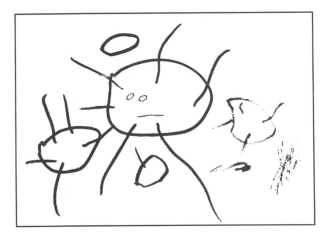

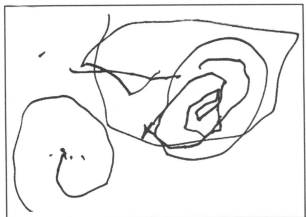

4 to 7 years

At this stage a child will draw pictures that tell a simple story. She begins to attach meaning to her lines, moving from just scribbling to imagination. This is a stage where parts of the total subject are represented symbolically. The child does not focus a great deal of attention on shape or proportion.

4 years

The four-year-old has the ability to draw circles and connect circles and lines. She can create "tadpole" people with faces, arms, and legs, with no body. Arms and legs are usually just lines coming out of the circle. She often draws unrealistically large objects on top for the head, and one limb larger than the other with exaggerated hands and feet. An awareness of gender difference is emerging, usually represented by longer hair. She can draw more than one object on a page with no realistic relationship to one another in size or context. She can also draw her environment: house, tree, sun with faces, clouds, rain. Interior and exterior objects may appear side by side.

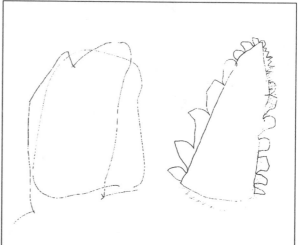

5 years

The five-year-old can now create a more complete figure, adding body parts, hair, and facial features. Images are drawn a little more realistically, although it is not unusual for limbs to be disproportionate, heads oversized, and lower torsos missing. Images are not as exaggerated as at the four-year-old level. There is a definite difference between girls and boys, with long hair for girls and short hair for boys. Boys are usually bigger. Rainbows, clowns, birds, and objects from the environment appear. Colors are used unrealistically.

6 years

The six-year-old can begin to draw pictures of a person, house, and tree. She begins to add details such as the sun, flowers, hats, or hair bows. The six-year-old is beginning a progression toward realism, drawing more distinct and representational details at each successive age level. The six-year-old also begins to use color more realistically. She now draws all the body parts, although they may still show distortion, for example, one leg larger than the other and/or one arm shorter than the other. She uses more details to differentiate between boys and girls. She now draws different sizes to represent age and importance. A six-year-old can also use fantasy in pictures to romanticize or compensate for feelings of longing, disappointment, etc.

7 to 10 years

This is a period of developing awareness and concern for realistic representations. Figures are readily recognizable to others. The concern with symmetry, placement, size, use of space, and creating an environment for the drawn objects become important. For example, a tree will be in a forest or next to a house with a ground line. She will attempt to make the tree proportionate to its surroundings. As the child develops through the years, the realistic aspects of her drawings become more sophisticated and complete. A seven-year-old will draw a house with all the essentials, without transparencies (an X-ray-like ability to see through solid walls). The eight-year-old, with her increased dexterity, will start perfecting the details with curtains, flowers, and movement of figures.

7 years

The seven-year-old can now draw without transparencies. Drawings begin to reflect the child's surroundings and more drawings will include a ground line and a horizon line. A child this age can also combine reality and fantasy. All figures are recognizable as male or female. Figures may face the front without showing movement, but movement will begin to be represented.

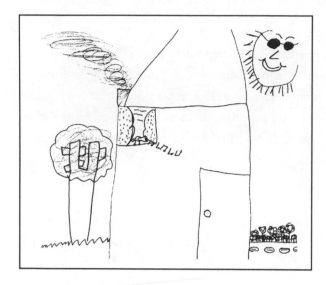

8 years

The eight-year-old begins to show her ability to handle pencils and crayons and draws realistically. She can use her imagination to create original responses to assignments and questions. An example is drawing a picture of herself in the rain or a picture of a fight, play, etc. She can express more movement and fantasy, while simultaneously showing more accurate proportions in relationship to objects in the drawing.

9 to 10 years

Children in this age group can represent ideas, draw people of different ages, and make clear gender distinction. They are becoming more aware of their bodies and are very interested in prepubescence, which causes some preadolescent anxiety. Secondary sexual features appear. People and objects in the environment are in realistic proportion to each other. Objects and people are illustrated in frontal and profile views and will show action. Baselines are elevated and ground lines are clearly drawn. Drawings show additional details, two and three dimensions, and perspective.

9 years

10 years

Preadolescent (11 to 12 years)

The drawings are fully developed and details are realistic and in perspective. In addition, doodles begin to express the child's focus on her emerging sexuality. By age eleven or twelve, children can also add exaggerated sexual characteristics to the human figure, for example large, rounded buttocks and breasts. She can use cartoons to voice and camouflage the sexual and identity concerns of this developmental stage.

11 years

12 years

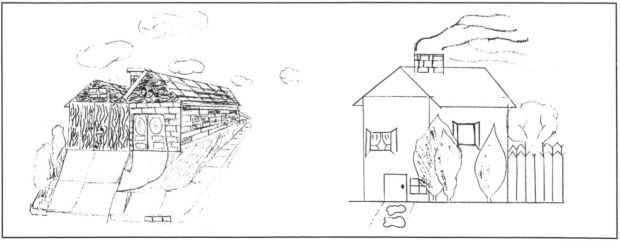

Summary

When examining children's drawings, you will not find a distinct line that delineates one age from the previous or subsequent age. Abilities spill over naturally from one age to another. Some abilities will seem regressed and others advanced. It is important to use common sense. It is also important to remember that one picture alone is not enough to determine the developmental level. A four-year-old child can draw a human being at a three-year-old level one day and a five-year-old level the next. *A pattern should be established in many drawings over a period of time.*

These brief descriptions of developmental stages by age are general guidelines to help establish whether a child is drawing in the normal range. A younger child often draws like her older siblings, but an older child who consistently draws at a much younger level bears observation.

You may often encounter drawings that are one level higher or lower than a child's age level. When this happens, it is important to know the child's living conditions, background, and family history to determine whether the child needs further observation. A very bright child with excellent motor skills drawing at a lower level is suspect if extenuating circumstances suggest emotional stress and if her behavior indicates some inappropriateness. If the same child is in a stable situation with little stress and she hates to draw, her bare-bones, minimalist drawing may be a normal response. However, her behavior should also be appropriate.

The examples of drawings at different age levels do not represent all the manifestations of each stage. They merely show a progression and the differences between levels as a child develops.

A word of caution!

Before we can judge a drawing we must scrupulously examine all relevant factors. While jumping to conclusions can be tempting, it is important to be thorough, scrutinizing every component of the drawing. Being consistent in analysis is also extremely helpful, and the following step-by-step approach can help you achieve this. A one-page summary of this approach appears on page 30.

A systematic approach consists of the following parts:

First Impressions
View the drawing in a global fashion

How does the drawing make you feel? The first impression is an important subjective piece of information. The feelings a drawing evokes in the viewer often mirror the artist's feelings. Famous artworks serve as excellent examples of first impressions. Monet's gardens and haystacks give a definite first impression of peacefulness. Renoir's portraits are distinctly soft and pink, emanating health. The first impressions of restlessness, pain, and anxiety in Van Gogh's starry skies and turbulent fields, and of terror in Munch's *The Scream* are exactly the opposite.

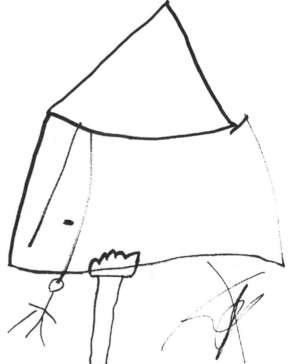

EXAMPLE

Figure 1 is an example of a first impression that sends up warning flags. Taylor, an eight-year-old boy, drew this picture of himself, a house, and a tree. At first glance, the drawing is immature and seems barren and detached with a floating quality. The empty, uninviting house has no windows and is almost triangular, like a tent. The door is incomplete so it can't be opened, and the roof is minimal. No ground line is present and the tree has no roots. The minimal stick figure has no facial features and is placed at an angle in the air. The drawing is not age appropriate and is incomplete and inadequate, giving an impression of inadequacy.

Figure 1 - Drawn by Taylor, age eight; average ability, behavior problem in school.

The specific characteristics supporting the first impression are . . .

➤ *No windows: hostile, no one can see in, isolated, withdraws from emotional contact.*

➤ *Almost triangular: four-year-old level.*

➤ *Incomplete door: can't go in.*

➤ *No ground line for house, person, and tree: lack of solid foundation, in the air.*

➤ *Minimal roof: illogical perspectives, breakdown in logical thinking, unimaginative.*

➤ *No chimney: lacking warmth, longs for nurturing.*

➤ *Minimalist, stick figure person: frequently drawn by sexually and physically abused children.*

➤ *No facial features: inaccessible.*

➤ *No roots for the tree: repressed emotions.*

➤ *Enclosed crown: encapsulated, outside forces cannot reach in.*

First impressions provide valuable information, but are not conclusive. *First impressions must be carefully supported by characteristics from the drawing.* Also keep in mind that first impressions can also be misleading. A talented young child with artistic ability can draw a beautiful picture that gives a positive first impression. Upon further scrutiny and careful examination of important characteristics, the drawing may include many signs of abuse, carefully veiled by the beauty and artistry of the drawing.

Log General Impressions

After noting your first impression, the following simple checklist of questions can help you sort out different aspects of a drawing. Some checklist items may not apply, but this systematic procedure can help you focus attention on relevant characteristics, draw attention to missing elements, and clarify details that support your first impression. Again, it is critical to note that *a single sign is not conclusive. The totality of all the signs, symbols, and characteris-* tics must be considered and generally support the hypothesis or conclusion.

CHECKLIST OF QUESTIONS

✓ *Was it a spontaneous or assigned drawing?*

✓ *Is it copied from another source? Does it come from the artist's imagination?*

✓ *Is it pleasant or disturbing? Is there a mood?*

✓ *How is it organized and composed? (complex, simple, orderly, chaotic)*

✓ *How is it drawn? (small, constricted, large, bold, structured, free)*

✓ *Where are the subjects/objects placed? What size are they?*

✓ *Does it show much imagination? Is it detailed or limited?*

✓ *What kind of shading was used? (excessive, artistic, patterns)*

✓ *What is the quality of the lines? (bold, faint, broken, continuous, uneven, jagged)*

✓ *What kind of pressure was used?*

✓ *Who is represented in the drawing? Is a significant person missing?*

✓ *Is it a self-portrait? (full face or profile, partial or whole body)*

✓ *What kind of figure is it? (representational, disjointed, fragmented, minimized, large, small)*

These questions help focus your attention on what the child may be saying about her inner world through the drawing—how she feels in relation to her peers and her family, how she shows her feelings, whether she is able to express freely or is restricted. Her drawing will reveal how ordered or chaotic her life may feel. These questions and thoughts will help point out expressions of anxiety, conflict, and upset.

Topics for Consideration

Context

When we look at a child's drawing we must look at it within the child's context. Analysis must be based on the child's:

➤ *age*

➤ *maturation*

➤ *emotional status*

➤ *social and cultural background*

➤ *other relevant history*

The drawing should also be consistent with the child's attitude and behavior. Disparities in the child's behavior, moods, patterns, etc., and her drawings can help inform us of what is happening within the child. When the drawings are disturbing and the child's behavior appears to be normal, certain questions regarding the drawings must be explored. Was the child taught to draw in a certain stylistic manner (e.g., shading all figures and areas, drawing suns with large spiky rays, knotholes, clouds with distinctive linings, distorted bodies)? Is the child copying styles of a sibling, friend, or someone seen on television? Are there consistent patterns in the drawings, or is her artistic style sporadic? If reasonable explanations are available, you can relax.

If the drawings are disturbing, you can presume that something is causing anxiety. The child's behavior may not be problematic, since some children are conscious about what is right and wrong and can control their behavior. Fortunately, it is more difficult to control the anxiety reflected in their drawings. Even the most benign subject matter—a house and a tree, for example—will reflect the disturbing feelings residing within the child.

When a child exhibits disturbing behaviors and draws disturbing pictures, the child is in stress and should be evaluated.

Consistency

Remember that one or two drawings are not enough to indicate trauma or problems. Trauma can only be determined from a series of drawings, drawn at different times with a consistent pattern. Each drawing must also contain a number of traits and characteristics, whose feeling and interpretation should be consistent with traits and characteristics in other drawings. For example:

1) If a child over the age of five draws a picture of herself with an extremely large head, large empty eyes, and abundant hair, it may be an indication of abuse and trauma. If subsequent drawings over a period of time do not have similar characteristics, we must assume that since a pattern does not exist, the one drawing is unique.

2) However, if the drawing was followed by other drawings with disturbing attributes★ (e.g., a tree with a heavily shaded trunk and a knothole in the center, a shaded house, a tree with a very shaded leaf system with wild swirls, persistence of shaded clouds, extremely large hands, large pointed teeth, fragmented body parts), it is safe to conclude that the child is clearly expressing distress. If these drawings appear in conjunction with acting out or acting in behaviors such as aggression, extreme passivity, feelings of inferiority, and a change in academic performance, there is sufficient information to recommend evaluation by a psychotherapist.

Always keep in mind the paramount consideration: More than a few isolated distinguishing features must appear over a period of time to warrant professional evaluation.

★ These are discussed in further detail in the "Characteristics" Chapter.

Behavior

When evaluating the initial psychological effects of child sexual abuse, researchers at Tufts University discovered a difference in the expression of symptomatic behavior relative to the age of the child. Children between four and six years of age exhibit less psychopathology than children ages seven to thirteen. Only 17 percent of the four- to six-year-olds met the criteria for "clinically significant pathology" compared to 40 percent of the seven- to thirteen-year-old group. (Tufts, 1984)

The younger group appears to turn fears inward, exhibiting inhibition, depression, and over-controlling behaviors. (Tufts, 1984) Since these features inhibit acting out behaviors, we are unable to recognize signs of trauma if we observe and examine only behavioral clues. It is our duty as caretakers to pay special attention to this group.

Fortunately for the older children, their angry, antisocial, and under-controlled behaviors are generally externalized and are more readily identified. However, a number of older children who do not exhibit these behaviors can still be classified as antisocial, so caretakers must be alert to any changes in their behavior. In these cases drawings, the result of a normal and enjoyable pastime, can provide a great deal of information regarding the child's state of mind and emotional life.

Some of the feelings and behaviors present in children who have been physically and sexually abused include:

➤ *aggression and antisocial behavior*
➤ *hostility*
➤ *active defiance*
➤ *disruptive behavior within the family*
➤ *quarreling or fighting with siblings or classmates*
➤ *changes in eating patterns*

➤ *sleep disturbances*
➤ *excessive masturbation*
➤ *depression (especially in girls)*
➤ *feelings of inferiority or a lack of worth*
➤ *guilt and shame*
➤ *delays in motor development*
➤ *learning problems*
➤ *hyperactive behaviors*
➤ *social-emotional delays*
➤ *role confusion*
➤ *sexual acting out*
➤ *self blame*
➤ *fear*
➤ *depersonalization*

If several of these behaviors coexist with drawings that show traits related to emotional, physical and/or sexual abuse, the child should definitely be evaluated.

Process

The artistic process itself can also give clues about anxieties and problems. The way the child draws the picture, for example, gives us important information. You can learn a great deal from the body language of the artist by watching the actual drawing process. It is important to notice how tightly she holds the crayons, her verbal and facial expressions, and her body posture during the process. Sometimes the child's attitude will change from passive to aggressive, mellow to angry, agitated to relieved. This is all valuable information. Again, keep in mind that meaningful interpretations cannot be made from a single sign, but depend on the combinations of indicators mentioned previously.

EXAMPLE

Seven-year-old John became very hostile in class and started picking fights with his male classmates. He could not contain himself. He soon began terrorizing the girls and would tease, hit, push, and swear at them whenever he was in close proximity. His drawings in class were heavily shaded, extremely messy, and very often totally disorganized.

It took several therapy sessions for John to settle down. He raged and used the plastic baseball bat to "kill" and "make dead" all the puppets, dinosaurs, dolls, and unbreakable miniature figures in the playroom. Finally, John was able to sit and draw. He continued to act out his aggression while drawing. He drew a large figure and a small figure and then started drawing a loop from the large figure to the smaller figure's buttocks. He would hit the buttocks with enough force to tear the paper. He continued to do this several times and then walked away. In the following session he drew the same picture and proceeded with the same behavior, at times making deep, guttural "grrrrrrrring" sounds. He identified the large figure as his uncle and the smaller figure as himself. He then switched and drew the loop from himself to the uncle with a loud "bang" and started "killing" his uncle. The subsequent investigation by Child Protective Services revealed that the uncle had sodomized John.

It would have been easy to overlook John's real situation since his pattern could have been diagnosed as a conduct disorder. Fortunately, although John was unable to verbalize his trauma because of the fear his uncle instilled in him, the drawings told us the story.

Placement

The placement of subjects and objects in the drawing tells us about the child. The paper represents the environment. The placement of the subjects and objects on the paper reflects the child's personality and shows how the child organizes her internal and external world. (Kaufman and Wohl, 1992)

A central placement of the drawn work is normal and suggests that the child is reasonably secure, self-directed, and self-centered. (Ogdon, 1977; Hammer, 1980) An image placed above the midline suggests that the child is striving toward unrealistic goals or expectations. An image that is positioned toward the bottom of the page may indicate concrete thinking and possibly depression. (Hammer, 1980; Jolles, 1964; Ogdon, 1977)

The right and left sides of the page also provide us with information. The right side suggests degrees of intellectualizing and self-control. It also represents behavior that is socially and future oriented. The left side is associated with emotional and impulsive individuals, self-absorbed and preoccupied with the past. (Jolles, 1971; Ogdon, 1977)

A child's drawing tells a story. The placement of subjects and objects can be quite literal. If the drawn image is placed on the paper so that it appears to float and is unconnected to anyone or anything, one can assume the artist is feeling that way. If the drawn person is removed from other people, the artist may be feeling isolated and disconnected. If furniture separates the person from the others, the artist may be needing some psychological space or may be feeling separated from others by something. *The place the artist puts herself in relation to others portrays the artist's perception of her importance to the drawn subjects and objects.* Whether she is first or last in line, the placement tells us how important the child feels in relation to the others.

23

It is also essential to notice inappropriately placed images. The child is sending a message. If a house and tree are drawn on the ground line and the child is floating in the air, you can infer that something is amiss with the child. If the child is the only one on the ground and the house and tree are in the air, something is definitely wrong in the household, her environment, or her perception.

Again, use common sense and consider the child's personal history, age, maturity, family, ethnicity, cultural background, economic conditions, medical history, and environment. A peculiar drawing in our culture may be perfectly normal in a different culture. If a child comes from a culture where everyone lives in houseboats or houses built on stilts, her perspective of home will be totally different from a typical California home.

EXAMPLE

Figure 2, a drawing by eight-year-old Lisa, shows unusual placement of important family members. Lisa was constantly getting into trouble at school. She was reprimanded for lying, fighting with schoolmates, and being rude to the teachers. Her behavior supported the anxiety represented in the drawing. Everyone is in the air. Lisa and her brother are sitting on the couch, without a ground line, watching TV. Her father is floating sideways and her mother is very small, floating almost out of the paper in the upper right-hand corner. The drawing represents what happened in the family when the parents were fighting. Both children try to zone out by watching TV. They are anxious, and the drawn eyes, incapable of seeing, clearly suggest they do not want to see what is happening around them. Both

are unable to make contact or move. Father starts raging and is irrational and mother threatens to leave, feeling ineffectual and disconnected. The parents are ambivalent about their relationship and their position in the family. Lisa is the largest figure in the drawing—she feels responsible for the family. Her acting out and aggressive behavior were masking her anxieties.

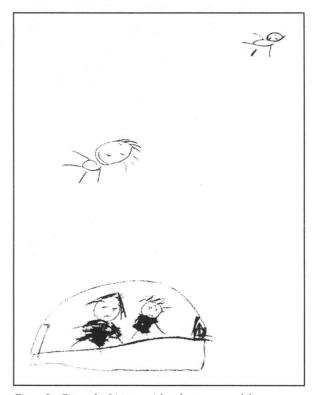

Figure 2 - Drawn by Lisa, age eight; above average ability.

First Impression

Bizarre, immature, floating

Specific characteristics:

➤ *Placement of parents floating sideways in the air*
➤ *No groundline for the couch (everything in the air)*
➤ *Unseeing eyes (not wanting to see)*
➤ *Children's bodies shaded (anxieties, possible sexual relevance)*
➤ *Heads very large (sexual, physical abuse)*

➤ *Messy hair (confused thinking)*

➤ *No hands (helplessness, sexual relevance)*

➤ *No feet (helplessness, cannot control environment, lack of ability to propel and direct herself in the world)*

➤ *No gender differentiation for mother*

➤ *Children larger than parents (parentified)*

Shading

Shading is possibly the most important clue in any drawing since it represents anxiety, agitation, and frustration. Any area in an object or subject that is especially highlighted by shading most likely symbolizes conflict. The heavier the shading, the greater the anxiety felt by the artist. The amount of anxiety is expressed by the darkness of the shading, and/or the swirl or agitated strokes of the pattern in the shading. If she feels a great deal of anxiety, stress, or anger, the artist may apply enough pressure on the drawing to punch a hole through the paper.

Heavy lines with shading in a particular area of the drawing or in subjects and/or objects can designate traumatized feelings. A knothole in a tree, for example, usually signifies trauma. If it is heavily lined and shaded, it reveals anxiety and shame. (Sometimes children learn to draw knotholes. One can assume these are insignificant if no other characteristics point to trauma.) A heavily lined and shaded cloud expresses an overbearing anxiety over the drawn area. If the person is heavily shaded, the artist is feeling a great amount of anxiety.

If all the drawn images reflect a general style and an evenness to the shading, it is important to determine whether this is a consistent style of drawing. Some children shade all their objects—this is obviously an artistic style. However, even if it is an artistic style, the artist still conveys her anxiety by shading heavily, using uneven, irregular strokes in conflicted areas.

Different patterns of shading also represent anxiety. Some examples of these patterns are heavy swirls, short choppy lines, heavy lines, agitated strokes, uneven areas of shading, jagged points, and scribbled curlicues. These patterns indicate stress and appear in the conflicted areas.

Repeated heavy pressure and bold lines on top of each other can also represent anxiety. Sometimes the artist will apply different colors on top of each other, often creating a messy blur. At times the artist may have great difficulty leaving the object and continues drawing until the object is a complete mess. This mess is associated with great anxiety.

EXAMPLE

Figure 3 is a drawing by eleven-year-old Carol. She came to therapy because she was depressed and extremely passive. She was very contained and reticent about talking about anything other than school. In the drawing she is shaded and enclosed in a shaded circle within a large, shaded, amoebic-looking circle. The lower part of the amoebic circle is heavily shaded. In the therapeutic process Carol disclosed that she was being physically and sexually abused by her stepfather. He would tie her hands to the clothes rod in the closet and place tacks under her feet, forcing her to stand on her tiptoes. Carol's mother did not protect her because she had turned the responsibility of discipline to the stepfather, who said that Carol was bad. When the mother was working as a nurse on the night shift, the stepfather would molest Carol and then tie her up. Since no one listened to her, she stopped talking and became emotionally unreachable.

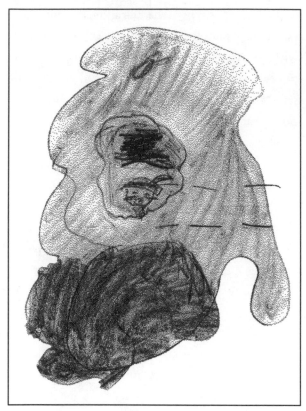

Figure 3 - Drawn by Carol, age eleven; depressed, passive, and withdrawn in school.

First Impression

Hiding and cartoon-like

Specific characteristics:

➤ *Whole drawing is shaded with areas of heavy shading (applied with different strokes, great deal of anxiety)*

➤ *Encapsulation, enclosure within an object or space (often drawn by sexually abused children)*

➤ *Abnormally tiny eyes without pupils (sexual relevance)*

➤ *Disproportionately large head (sexual relevance)*

➤ *Body without lower half (sexual relevance)*

➤ *Compartmentalized (isolation)*

➤ *Animal-like self-representation (does not feel human, primitive basic feelings)*

➤ *Very heavy shaded cloud hanging directly over her*

Size of Subjects and Objects

The size of a figure represents self-esteem. An overly large figure that fills up most of the space indicates infantile grandiosity. The figure covers up and compensates for the artist's feelings of powerlessness and ineffectiveness. A tiny figure depicts a person with feelings of inadequacy, inferiority, low self-esteem, and a weak ego. (In a normal 8½-by-11 inch sheet of paper, small is less than 2 inches and large is 9 inches or more.)

Different sizes of people give us an idea of the importance of the people depicted by the artist. It also shows the relationships in the family, with others, and to objects. If the child in the drawing is larger than the mother or father, the child is sending a message that she is in the parent or power role. There is a direct relationship between large and important, and small and powerless.

Subject Matter

Appropriateness of subject matter is important. For example, drawing witches or devils is normal in a Halloween picture, but inappropriate in a Christmas drawing. What is the artist trying to convey?

When a child is asked to draw a picture of herself and she draws an animal or her friends, or ignores the request and draws something that seems irrelevant, the child is sending a message. When this happens you can ask for more information about the drawing in a manner that shows interest rather than inquisition. The child will usually tell what is on her mind directly or in a story or fairy tale mode.

EXAMPLE

No matter what directions I gave Sarah, age ten, she kept drawing pictures of a man hanging upside down. She was unable to talk about the drawing or make up a story about the drawing. She just said she "had to draw it." Eventually her nightmares became clearer and she finally "saw" a scene when she was very young. It was at a family summer camp and a man was found hung, upside down. This scene was corroborated by her mother and Sarah was able to repair the trauma.

Details

Normal drawings have the usual composite of essential details to complete the picture. Assessing the details that are included or excluded in the drawing can facilitate the viewer's understanding of conflicts, dangers, and problems. The artist's possible strengths and weaknesses can also be attributed. For example, if a house has a fence around it, and no door, the artist is sending a very strong "keep out" message. The artist is making a statement of vulnerability, of being withdrawn and isolated, protecting herself from others.

Too many or too few details is cause for concern. Abused children often draw with excessive details. Many abused children, whose family lives lack organization and tend to be chaotic, feel a very strong need to structure the environment. This is an effort to gain some control over an element in their lives.

Inadequately detailed drawings, according to Hammer (1980), suggest inner emptiness, depression, and low energy level. Since a normal child does not add irrelevant details to a drawing or omit important ones, you can use common sense to determine what the artist is communicating.

The details and their placement add valuable insight. As mentioned earlier, the placement of objects is often literal. When a child is traumatized by abuse and feels fragmented, her feelings are reflected in several ways. Her details may be placed on the paper without any logical reason and order. These details have no coherent theme so the drawing is confusing and fragmented, much like the child.

EXAMPLE

Figure 4 is an example of excessive detail. I asked Jane, age seven, to draw a picture of a tree. She put the tree on the far right-hand side of the paper with a knothole and very agitated shaded trunk. She added a horse with flowers and a ground line of woven grass, diverting attention away from the tree. She had been molested by the gardener who came to the house once a week. When Jane told her mother, the gardener was reported to Child Protective Services. Jane's mother was filled with guilt for not protecting Jane and became seriously dysfunctional for a short period of time. Jane began feeling her mother's anxiety. She became aggressive and began having learning difficulties. She needed structure and order in her life to feel protected. When the mother stablilized, Jane began her healing process.

Figure 4 - Drawn by Jane, age seven; above average in abilities, agitated, unable to focus in class.

First Impression

Pastoral (tree drawing)

Specific characteristics:

➤ *Details, the colorful flowers with carefully woven grass and a horse in center stage (needing structure as well as detracting from tree)*

➤ *Heavy and chaotic shading on trunk (anxieties)*

➤ *Heavily shaded knothole (trauma associated with shame)*

➤ *Overly large branch structure (concerned with having needs met by others)*

➤ *Scribbled, disorganized crown (impulsiveness, confused thinking and value structure)*

➤ *Crown down over the trunk (nothing within, driven by others)*

➤ *No roots (repressed emotions)*

➤ *Placement of tree on right side (male dominance, controlling tendencies)*

Erasures

Erasures are important when they make the drawing worse from overworking the detail. This usually happens when the child is dealing with conflict, uncertainty, indecisiveness, or fear of not "doing it right." Erasures reflect feelings of general dissatisfaction and self-distrust. Excessive erasures are likely to emerge in the drawings of a traumatized child, since trauma often causes the disintegration of a positive sense of self, resulting in self-distrust and low self-esteem. (Kaufman and Wohl, 1992)

Color

J. N. Buck, E. F. Hammer, and I. A. Jolles have examined the meaning and significance of color. They came to the conclusion that color has significance, but in general, color usage is so subjective that there is no consensus of possible interpretations. Children use different colors for many feelings. No feelings are consistently tied with a certain color. For example, blue and red can be happy, sad,

quiet, or peaceful. Children often choose a color just because they "like it." Color creates a mood, but we must be careful not to attribute our own subjective feelings and interpretations to the drawing.

Subjects: Person, House, Tree

Human Figure

The next step is to look at the human figure systematically. A systematic approach makes it easier to notice troubling and missing characteristics. At times, an obvious characteristic will be absent but goes unnoticed because a dramatic characteristic has overshadowed it. In one picture, for example, an overabundance of elaborate and colorful hair distracted from the omission of a torso and neck. The hair attracted so much attention that the lack of a body was unnoticed until viewed using a checklist.

The easiest approach to analyzing the body is to start from the top and go down to the feet. Ask yourself questions about each body part using the following list. The aspects following each name are prompts to trigger questions to yourself about the characteristic you are examining.

✓ *Head (disproportionately large or small)*

✓ *Hair (abundant, coiffured, scribbled, scant, absent, missing on top)*

✓ *Eyes (large, small, empty, without pupils, crazy-looking, crossed)*

✓ *Mouth (absent, emphasized, cosmetic or minimally represented, open, closed)*

✓ *Nose (absent, tiny, large, nostrils shown)*

✓ *Ears (prominent, absent, reinforced)*

✓ *Teeth (large, pointed, mouthful, rounded)*

✓ *Trunk (absent, tiny, smaller than head, emphasized, organs or navel visible, sturdy, frail)*

✓ *Breasts (absent, emphasized, firm, drooping, abundant)*

✓ *Crotch (excessive attention, erasures, shading)*

✓ *Genitalia (suggested, explicitly shown, exaggerated, covered by an object)*

✓ *Arms (large, muscular, absent, sticklike, long, short)*

✓ *Hands (excessively large, small, open, closed)*

✓ *Fingers (absent, spike or clawlike)*

✓ *Legs (two or more, wide apart, close together, sturdy, spindly)*

✓ *Feet (absent, large, small, moving, static)*

✓ *Clothing (belts, zippers, bra tops, shorts, jewelry, adornments)*

House

Essential elements: door, windows, walls, roof, chimney. By the time a child is six, a basic house should have one door, one window, a roof, a chimney, and walls. Pay special attention to any omission. (Kaufman and Wohl, 1992; Oster and Gould, 1987)

The size of the house, the placement, the shading, and the details the artist found important to include or exclude are all important characteristics to note. What is the general impression of the house? How does it look? What mood does it convey? Is it accessible? Does it look pleasant or does it have an empty feeling? Is the house complete? Any missing element indicates a message from the artist.

Figure 1 can also be used as an example for the house. It is an inadequate house—none of the bare essentials are represented completely and well.

Tree

Essential elements: roots, trunk, branches, and leaves. By age seven, a child can draw a tree with a trunk and at least one branch. After age seven, trees are less subject to developmental changes.

The tree can also be a symbolic representation of the artist. Like the human figure and the house, the tree gives the viewer information about the artist. The shading and the drawing process will offer clues to the artist's emotional state.

The size of the tree, the placement, and the relationship between the tree and the house or person is analyzed the same way as the human figure. Be aware of the impression the tree gives. Are the branches and leaves tight and constricted, or are they very loose? Is the trunk sturdy or spindly and off-center? Is the tree appropriate to the drawing? Is the tree appropriate in size and placement?

The example shown previously in Figure 4 can also be used for the tree. When I asked Jane to draw a tree, she put the tree on the very edge of the paper. She then drew a horse, placing the horse in the center with many flowers. She was clearly trying to distract me from herself and her trauma by wanting me to focus on the horse. She had been doing the same thing with her molestation. The tree is very shaded and strongly scribbled. Jane's branches and leaf system have a chaotic feel to them and some almost reach the flowers. A knothole right in the center can hardly be seen. These characteristics can indicate molestation. On a subjective level, Jane was feeling confused and wanted to hide.

Summary

➤ An alarming drawing is important for a teacher or caregiver to notice, but by itself does not indicate trauma or problems.

➤ An alarming drawing is a cue to watch for other alarming signs or symptoms: a series of similar drawings, a change in the child's behavior, a change in school performance, etc.

➤ When you first look at a drawing, allow yourself a first impression. Notice your own feelings. Separate the drawing from yourself.

➤ Use the systematic checklists to determine whether or not a drawing conveys any problems, stress, and/or anxiety.

Basic Steps in Analyzing Drawings

1. First and global impression

Note personal feelings about the drawing.

See Checklist of Questions to sharpen different aspects (p. 20).

2. Incorporate child's personal history; e.g. age, social, cultural, emotional...

3. Are there discrepancies? *(p. 5)*

4. How is the drawing presented?

Placement of objects, shading, size of subjects and objects, subject matter, details (pp. 23-26)

5. What condition is the drawing in?

Erasures, tears, messy

6. Focus on the subject: Person, House and/or Tree

   a. Person *Checklist (p. 28, 29)*

   • *What characteristics attract attention? Record the interpretation (p. 35–46).*

   • *Start with the head and go down to the feet systematically.*

   • *Record all interpretations of any characteristic that merit noting.*

   • *Look at the whole person. Has your first impression changed? Is your first impression validated?*
     Are there discrepancies?

   b. House *(p. 29)*

   • *Are the essential elements presented?*

   • *What characteristics attract attention?*

   • *Check each essential element and note interpretations of questionable characteristics (p. 48–52).*

   c. Tree *(p. 29)*

   • *Are all the essential elements there?*

   • *What characteristics draw attention?*

   • *Check each essential element and note interpretations for questionable elements in the drawing (p. 53–56).*

   d. Details *(p. 27)*

   • *Are details used appropriately? Check the Details section in the Characteristics chapter (p. 57–59).*

7. Review all your notes

Are there groupings of similar interpretations?

8. Check the behavioral list *(p. 22)*

If the behaviors and the drawing match up, save the drawing with your notes. Begin collecting the drawings to determine if there is a consistent pattern.

CHARACTERISTICS

> Characteristic: *An element, aspect, or part of a drawing that symbolically represents a feeling or emotion of the artist. It can be as simple as a part of the body, a house, or a tree, or more complex, for example the way in which these parts are represented (e.g., shading, placement, process, lines, and pressure).*

Artists use characteristics to symbolically convey information about their internal state and feelings. The representations of figures and objects and the way they are drawn give us clues that help us interpret the artist's message. An example of a characteristic is a body part on a drawn figure. The body part's inappropriate size, heavy shading, omission, or strange shape, make the characteristic unique.

These characteristics gain significance when they are represented in a way that deviates from the norm. An example might be the use of shading. One can usually recognize anxiety in a drawing through the use of shading. The more intense the shading, the more intense the anxiety. When certain areas in the person are shaded, they represent the area of concern and anxiety. Shading in the face, for example, can mean that the person is seriously disturbed or has a poor self concept. If the genital areas are shaded, then those are areas of conflict and anxiety which may indicate possible sexual abuse or sexual concerns. Shading is an important clue to locating the areas of concern.

Shading can have different textures, and the more disturbed the texture, the more anxiety the child is experiencing. Textures can be represented by overlays of color, daubing color in splotches, swirls, scribbles, distinct lines drawn within a subject matter, circles, and any other ingenious method

a child can think of. Because shading is so obvious, it is usually the first clue we notice that points to a potential problem.

All these characteristics should be viewed with the preceding chapter, "Analyzing the Drawing," in mind. The placement of the objects, the size, the appropriateness, the details of the characteristic, and the process through which the drawing evolved all provide important information. Within this framework, the important characteristic to note will become evident. To determine whether the child might be potentially at risk, the same message must appear in a series of drawings in different subjects and objects.

As you examine the characteristics, it is crucial to keep in mind the age and developmental level of the child. A four-year-old child is not going to draw a house with all the essentials. However, a seven-year-old child is capable of doing so. Age appropriateness is imperative for an accurate assessment. An example of this would be an eleven-year-old child drawing pictures with transparencies. This is normal for a child under seven, but at eleven the child normally draws realistic representations.

Sources

This chapter is a compilation of essential characteristics, along with the meaning or interpretation attributed to these characteristics by the major art therapy experts. The interpretations were derived from tens of thousands of drawings, from both normal children in normal settings and abused children in shelters. The characteristics in this chapter are those represented outside the norm, grouped in six categories for the reader's ease of use:

1) General
2) Person
3) Sexual
4) House
5) Tree
6) Miscellaneous Details

They have been sorted in this manner since person, tree, and house are the primary subjects that children are asked to draw as they are being evaluated.

As repeated footnotes would make the chapter too cluttered, I am presenting all authors whose works formed the basis of the list here:

K. Bolander; A. Browne and D. Finkelhor; J. N. Buck; A. Burgess, M. McCausland and W. Wolbert; R. C. Burns; F. Cohen and R. Phelps; F. Culbertson and A. Revel; J. Di Leo; E. F. Hammer; R. Hibbard and R. Hoekelman and K. Roghmann; I. A. Jolles; B. Kaufman and A. Wohl; S. Kelley; M. Klepsch and L. Logie; C. Koch; E. Koppitz; K. Machover; C. Malchiodi; D. Ogdon; G. D. Oster and P. Gould; C. Saarni and V. Azara; C. Stember; and V. Van Hutton.

These authors' works contain detailed information regarding the characteristics and traits. Titles are listed in the Bibliography and characteristics associated with the authors are listed in the Appendix.

General Characteristics in a Drawing

DETAILS ➤ inadequate details
- *inner emptiness, low energy level, depression*

➤ excessive details
- *need to structure environment*
- *sexual abuse*

ERASURES (WHEN DRAWING IS WORSE BECAUSE OF IT)
➤ conflicted issues, uncertainty, indecisiveness, generalized dissatisfaction with self, traumatized, need to be perfect

➤ anxiety, internal stress

LINES ➤ broken, sketchy, small, wavering lines
- *insecure, shy, uncertain, hesitation, indecision, fearfulness*
- *incipient ego disintegration*

➤ heavy, reinforced
- *inner tension, tendency to act out aggressively, forcefulness*

➤ rigid straight (rulerlike) lines
- *obsessive-compulsive, rigid, aggressive tendency*

PLACEMENT ➤ high, top of page
- *use fantasy to achieve goals*
- *striving, difficult to reach goals*
- *tendency to withdraw*
- *fear and avoidance of others*

➤ low, bottom of page
- *insecurity, inadequacy, dependency*
- *reality-oriented, concrete thinking, need for support*

➤ above midline
- *striving toward unrealistic goals or expectations*

➤ central
- *normal*

➤ right side
- *structured, intellectual*
- *future-oriented*
- *male-oriented*

➤ left side
  • *emotional, unstructured*
  • *tendency to impulsiveness*
  • *past-oriented*
  • *feminine*

➤ angle (15 degrees or more)
  • *insecurity*

PRESSURE

➤ consistent
  • *normality and stability*

➤ heavy (may tear paper)
  • *traumatized*

➤ light
  • *hesitation, fearfulness*

SHADING (NOT TO BE CONFUSED WITH STYLISTIC SHADING)

➤ anxiety, agitation, preoccupation, and fixation
➤ area of conflict

TRANSPARENCIES (X-RAY-LIKE ABILITY TO SEE THROUGH OPAQUE OBJECTS DRAWN BY CHILDREN OVER SEVEN YEARS OF AGE)

➤ disturbed, emotionally pathological
➤ regression to primary process thinking
➤ immaturity, impulsive acting out
➤ mirror children's feelings that they are transparent
➤ focus on the locale of the trauma or distress

Person (Whole)

TINY FIGURE ➤ extreme insecurity, depression

➤ ineffectiveness

➤ feelings of inadequacy

➤ low self-esteem

➤ anxious

➤ inferiority

➤ withdrawal from environment

➤ sexual relevance

LARGE FIGURE

➤ expansiveness

➤ poor inner control

➤ overcompensates for powerlessness

CONSTRICTED ➤ stressed

FIGURE SLANTING MORE THAN 15 DEGREES

➤ instability, insecure

➤ mental imbalance

POOR INTEGRATION OF PARTS

➤ low frustration and tolerance, impulsiveness

SHADING—ANXIETY, CONFLICT, DISTURBANCE

➤ face—seriously disturbed

➤ arms—aggressive impulses

➤ body—feelings, emotional conflict

➤ genital area—possible sexual abuse, anxiety and conflict concerning sexuality

LACK OF DIFFERENCE IN GENDER

➤ likely indicator of sexual trauma

PROFILE ➤ hesitancy to face and communicate with others

➤ serious withdrawal tendencies

FEMALE FIGURES DRAWN BY MALES

➤ emphasis on hair, breasts, and bare legs

• *strong sexual impulses are conveyed*

➤ asexual female body (e.g., mother does not look any different from a boy or a man)

• *denies sexuality in that person*

MATURITY — AGE REPRESENTATION
> older or younger
  • *sexual relevance*

Parts of the Body (in Alphabetical Order)
Arms

Used to reach, hold, touch, change, or control surrounding environment. Arms and hands refer to ego development and social adaptation. We perform skills and explore our environment, both personal and interpersonal, and make contact with persons through our arms and hands.

OMISSION (BOYS OVER SIX AND GIRLS OVER FIVE)
> inability to manipulate and control environment
> strong need to regulate impulses through superego control
> inadequacy, helplessness
> inability to make contact
> passive, can do nothing
> guilt over hostility or sexuality
> hostility
> sexual relevance

LACK OF ATTACHMENT TO BODY
> hopeless, inadequate

FLIMSILY CONNECTED
> difficulty in ego development and socialization

HEAVILY SHADED
> guilt regarding sexual impulses
> aggressive impulses

NOTICEABLE DIFFERENTIAL TREATMENT OF ARMS–LENGTH, SIZE, SHAPE
> suggestive of sexual abuse
> aggression, hostility

LARGE—DISPROPORTIONATELY
> aggression, hostility

SHORT (ABOVE WAIST)
> tendency to withdraw
> turning inward
> attempt to inhibit impulses
> ineptitude in reaching others

➤ inadequate

➤ limited ability to reach, touch, and receive nurturing

LONG (NEAR KNEES)

➤ ambition for achievement or for acquisition

➤ reaching out toward others

➤ aggressively seeking out the environment

➤ externally directed tendencies

➤ need for mother's protection

➤ wanting to control anger

➤ interpersonal reluctance

FOLDED OVER CHEST

➤ hostile or suspicious

OUTWARD REACHING

➤ desire for contact

TRANSPARENT

➤ confused thinking, way of reaching out is distorted and unrealistic

ARMS HOVERING OVER SHOULDERS

➤ ward off intruders, trying to protect self

PRESSED CLOSELY AND RIGIDLY AGAINST THE BODY

➤ reluctance to get involved with others

REINFORCED ARMS, EXAGGERATED, EMPHASIZED MUSCLES

➤ hostility, aggression

HELD BEHIND BACK

➤ wanting to control anger, interpersonal reluctance

Beard

SHADED, AGITATED, MESSY-LOOKING

➤ sexual drives

➤ sexual relevance

SHADED FACIAL HAIR, E.G., GOATEE, BEARD

➤ trepidation of male sexuality

Body (Trunk)

BOX SHAPE (ROBOTLIKE)

➤ successful restraint, keeping impulses at bay

➤ emotional disturbance, acting out tendencies

➤ depersonalized, dehumanized, emotional numbness

➤ cerebrally controlled, rational, unemotional

➤ possible sexual abuse

OMISSION   ➤ denial of body drives and feelings

OPEN TRUNK (OUTLINE NOT COMPLETE)

➤ outer shell, open and vulnerable

➤ body is empty of feelings, powerless

➤ no closure between legs, legs continue into trunk
  • *sexual relevance*

BIZARRE, SCATTERED PARTS, POORLY INTEGRATED, BARELY RECOGNIZABLE

➤ seriously disturbed child

➤ traumatized, sexually abused

MINIMALIST (STICK FIGURE)

➤ insecure

➤ depressed

BODY PARTS COVERED BY OBJECT

➤ sexual relevance

SHADED BODY

➤ sexual relevance

ENLARGEMENT, EXAGGERATION OF BODY PARTS

➤ preoccupation with function

POOR INTEGRATION OF PARTS IN THE BODY

➤ low frustration tolerance and impulsivity

Breasts

EMPHASIZED, PRESENT IN DRAWINGS

➤ sexual relevance

Chest

Holding tank for feelings.

CONSTRICTED

➤ cover up and restrict emotions

Ears

CONSPICUOUS

➤ paranoid, suspicious attitudes

OMISSION   ➤ not wanting to hear

REINFORCED — DOUBLE LINES-LARGE
> ➤ guarded, suspicious, and distrustful

Eyes

LARGE (UNUSUALLY)
> ➤ suspicious, alert to danger, lack of trust

TINY   ➤ inhibited
> ➤ strong visual curiosity linked with guilt
> ➤ withdrawn, inaccessible

QUALITY OF EYES
> ➤ grotesque—terror, horror, fear
> ➤ vacant—not seeing, not wanting to see

WITHOUT PUPILS, ABNORMALLY TINY, HIDDEN BY DARK GLASSES, OR OMISSION
> ➤ possible sexual abuse

CROSSED EYES
> ➤ confused, crazy feeling
> ➤ sexual relevance

SIDEWAYS GLANCE
> ➤ suspicion and paranoid tendencies

CLOSED EYES
> ➤ withdrawn, inaccessible

ONE EYE   ➤ lack of trust, alert to danger, suspicious

DARK, REINFORCED OUTLINE
> ➤ lack of trust, alert to danger, suspicious

Face

MASKLIKE   ➤ emotional numbing
> ➤ hidden feelings

DARK LINE AROUND FACE
> ➤ strong effort to maintain control over upsetting thoughts

FACIAL FEATURES
> ➤ dim, faint, barely visible
>> • *withdrawn, inaccessible*

➤ strong, reinforced, heavy, dark, emphasized features
  • *aggression, hostility*

SHADING ➤ seriously disturbed, poor self-concept

Feet

Degree of groundedness and interpersonal mobility.

LONG, ELONGATED

➤ striving for security or virility

➤ sexual relevance

TINY ➤ dependency, blunted feelings

➤ withdrawal, guarded accessibility

LARGE ➤ sexual relevance

OMISSION (BOYS OVER NINE, GIRLS OVER SEVEN)

➤ lack of independence

➤ helplessness, lack of "sure footing"

➤ cannot control environment

➤ lack of ability to propel and direct oneself in the world

TIPTOES ➤ conveys feelings of inadequacy

➤ tenuously balanced, struggling to maintain balance

Fingers

Ability to manipulate environment, world.

LONG AND SPIKE-LIKE

➤ aggressive, hostile

ENCLOSED BY LOOP OR SINGLE DIMENSION

➤ wish to suppress aggressive impulse

OMISSION ➤ problems relating to others

➤ effort to contain aggressive impulses

WITHOUT HANDS

➤ aggression, hostility

Genitals and Secondary Sexual Features

Unless children have had sexual abuse prevention education either at home or at school, *it is extremely rare for children to draw genitals, with the exception of sexually abused children.* When genitals appear, you must *look carefully at all the other signs in the drawings for corroboration.*

PENIS, VAGINA

> ➤ strong possibility of sexual abuse

BREASTS ON CHESTS DRAWN BY YOUNG GIRLS

> ➤ indicator suggesting sexual violation

DRAWING OF THE OPPOSITE SEX

> ➤ emphasis on hair, breasts, bare legs
>   • *age-inappropriate sexual concerns*
>   • *strong sexual impulses conveyed*
>   • *sexual relevance*
> ➤ emphasis on zipper of pants or shorts
>   • *conflict about concealment and exhibition of male body*
>   • *anxiety regarding sexuality*

Hair

HEAVILY SHADED

> ➤ anxiety
> ➤ impulses breaking through

MESSY HAIR ➤ thinking is confused

TIGHTLY CURLED AND SCRIBBLED OR SHADED

> ➤ anxiety about own thoughts

LONG AND WILD

> ➤ indulges impulses to immediate gratification

THINNING AT CROWN, LONG HAIR AT SIDES

> ➤ anxiety about own thoughts
> ➤ sexual abuse

REINFORCED HAIRLINE

> ➤ struggling to contain impulses through ego defenses

OMISSION ➤ males–possible conflict of male identity

JAGGED BANGS, HAIR SPIKED (PUNK STYLE)

> ➤ impulses breaking through

SHADED HAIR ON A REPRESENTED MALE PERSON, I.E., FATHER, ETC.
> ➤ trepidation about male sexuality

SHADED FACIAL HAIR, GOATEE, BEARD
> ➤ trepidation of male sexuality
> ➤ sexual relevance

EXCESSIVE, EXAGGERATED HAIR
> ➤ physical abuse

HAIR ON ARMS, LEGS, AND/OR BODY
> ➤ sexual relevance

Hands

ABSENCE OF WELL–DEFINED HANDS
> ➤ helplessness, cannot control or manipulate the environment
>   • *"take care of me"*
> ➤ sexual relevance

LARGE
> ➤ acting out behavior
> ➤ angry, aggressive, hostile
> ➤ impulsive

TINY OR MISSING FINGERS
> ➤ inadequate, insecure

CUT OFF HAND
> ➤ troubled, inadequate
> ➤ aggressive

OMISSION
> ➤ inability to make contact
> ➤ inability to "do things"
> ➤ prohibition of making contact with environment, interpersonal relationships, and acting on personal needs
> ➤ cut off from connecting
> ➤ inadequate and insecure
> ➤ sexual relevance

HIDDEN
> ➤ presence of guilty feelings

MITTENLIKE HANDS
> ➤ repression of aggressive feelings with outward appearance of compliance

HANDS COVERING GENITAL REGION

> sexual relevance

FISTS, CLENCHED

> hostility, aggression

Head

Associated with ego.

LARGE   ➤ preoccupation with fantasy life, focus on mental life

VERY LARGE, A QUARTER OF THE SIZE OF THE PERSON

> sexual abuse, physical abuse

SMALL   ➤ obsessive-compulsive, intellectual inadequacy

> impulses are winning battle for control and overwhelming ability to use intellect

> sexual relevance

BACK TO VIEWER

> paranoid or schizoid tendencies

ENLARGED HEAD WITH REINFORCED HAIRLINE

> struggle to contain impulses through ego defenses

HOLE   ➤ damaged, no good

> feels stupid, no brains

PRESENCE OF EXTRANEOUS CIRCLES

> suggestive of sexual abuse

DISCONNECTED

> separated from feelings, emotions

Legs

Depict feelings of groundedness and mobility.

OMISSION   ➤ constricted, possible castration anxiety

> sexual relevance

SIZE DIFFERENCE

> mixed feelings regarding independence

LONG   ➤ striving for autonomy

SHORT   ➤ emotional immobility

PERSON

SINGLE THIN LINE, STICKLIKE, FEEBLE
> ➤ powerlessness
> ➤ vulnerability

TIGHTLY HELD TOGETHER
> ➤ holding back sexual energy

WIDE STANCE
> ➤ suggestion of overt aggression

LIGHT, SKETCHY LINE PRESSURE
> ➤ sexual relevance

GROSS ASYMMETRY
> ➤ aggressive

CUT OFF ➤ cannot move

Lips
CUPID'S BOW MOUTH
> ➤ sexual relevance

Mouth
LARGE AND OPEN
> ➤ intense neediness

OVERLY EMPHASIZED
> ➤ immaturity, oral–aggressive

VERY LARGE ➤ orally erotic

SHORT HEAVY LINE
> ➤ aggressive, hostile

Neck
Connection between intellectual and bodily drives.

**OMISSION OR BREAK BETWEEN HEAD AND BODY
(BOYS OVER TEN, GIRLS OVER NINE)**
> ➤ deployment of defense mechanism of isolation
> ➤ isolation by separating ideas from the feelings
> ➤ emotional numbing
> ➤ difficulty with bodily impulses and concerns

THIN, ELONGATED NECK
- ➤ associated with feelings of body weakness and organ inferiority
- ➤ compensatory drive towards physical power and aggression
- ➤ separates thoughts from emotions
- ➤ struggle, difficult to maintain control over bodily concerns, impulses, and anxieties
- ➤ sexual relevance

THICK, ELONGATED NECK
- ➤ concern with morals

THICK, SHORT NECK
- ➤ aggressive, hostile

WEAK NECK
- ➤ fragile connection between torso and head
- ➤ poor modulation between thoughts and feelings

Nose
LARGE, HEAVILY OUTLINED, SHADED, EMPHASIZED
- ➤ sexual relevance

Nostrils
EMPHASIZED ➤ aggression, hostility

Pelvic Area
EMPHASIZED ➤ sexual relevance

Shoulders
UNEQUAL ➤ emotionally unstable

LARGE, OVERSIZED, PADDED
- ➤ preoccupied with the perceived need for strength
- ➤ acting strong
- ➤ aggression, hostility

SQUARED, FLATTENED
- ➤ overly defended, hostile towards others
- ➤ carrying burden, defended

TINY ➤ inferiority

SKINNY, NARROW
- ➤ weakness, self-doubt

PERSON

Teeth

Aggressiveness (orally related).

SHARP, POINTED

➤ aggressive acting out

EXPOSED TEETH

➤ anger

ENLARGED, ROUNDED TEETH

➤ defensive stance

➤ hopeless

Waist

DROPPED WAIST

➤ connotes sexual tensions

WIDE BELT ➤ inner struggle to maintain control over sexual drives

Sexual

Characteristics frequently drawn by sexually and physically abused children:

HEADS WITHOUT BODIES

BODIES WITHOUT LOWER HALF

DISORGANIZATION OF BODY PARTS, DEFORMED BODY IMAGE, FRAGMENTATION

ENCAPSULATION OF A PERSON
> ➤ enclosure within an object or space

DISPROPORTIONATELY LARGE HEAD

EYES WITHOUT PUPILS (BLIND EYES), ABNORMALLY TINY, HIDDEN BY DARK GLASSES OR OMITTED ENTIRELY

GEOMETRIC, BOXLIKE BODY

BIZARRE, SCATTERED BODY PARTS, POORLY INTEGRATED

MINIMALIST (STICK FIGURE)

COMPARTMENTALIZED (SEPARATED BY LINES, PUT INTO BOXES, NO CONNECTION IN THE DRAWING)
> ➤ expresses lack of communication and isolation

PERSON DRAWN SEPARATED BY FURNITURE
> ➤ need for psychological space

MISSING HANDS AND ARMS

OVEREMPHASIS OF THE MOUTH, LARGE AND ORAL

Items or features usually not found in normal drawings of the human figure drawn by children:

TINY OR LARGE HEAD

CROSSED EYES

TEETH

SHORT OR LONG ARMS

BIG HANDS

CLINGING ARMS

LEGS PRESSED TOGETHER

GENITALS

MONSTERLIKE FINGERS

CLOUDS, SNOW, OR RAIN

House

The drawing of a house tends to show what is happening in the child's home and the interpersonal dynamics being experienced in that setting. The house can show activity with busy people and inviting rooms, or look desolate and bleak with no one around.

The house can also be a symbolic representation of the child and how the child feels about herself. The house reflects body image, maturity, adjustment, and emotional stability. (Buck, 1981; Hammer, 1980) When it is viewed as representing the person, it can be interpreted by using the characteristics as symbols. For example, if the house is shaded with no door and no windows, it is safe to assume that the child is anxious and withdrawn. The child is not letting anyone in and is not coming out at that time.

By the time the child is six, the basic house must have one door, one window, one wall, a roof, and a chimney. (Kaufman and Wohl, 1992; Oster and Gould, 1987) If an essential component is missing from the house, its omission provides information for the viewer. For example, a missing wall can show us that the child may be vulnerable, unprotected, or is not feeling contained.

Irrelevant considerations are shrubs, flowers, birds, and other details that fill up the drawing rather than the essential house itself. If a child draws an incomplete house and fills the drawing with irrelevant details, one can assume that the child feels insecure and incomplete and needs to control the environment.

House (Whole)

GLOBAL IMPRESSION
- friendly, pleasant, welcoming
- unfriendly, foreboding, frightening
- home you would go into or stay away from

SMALL HOUSE (DISPROPORTIONATE)
- sense of losing self when in a relationship
- withdrawn, guarded accessibility

LARGE HOUSE
- aggression, hostility
- overcompensates

STRUCTURE
- open-ended, no designating line between roof and walls, etc.
  - *boundaries are virtually nonexistent*

TRIANGULAR HOUSE (NORMAL FOR FOUR-YEAR-OLD)
- possible lag in cognitive development
- inability to interact adequately with the world
- behaviors and responses are restricted

Perspective

The house is drawn to look as if the artist is looking up from below the house or looking down from above.

FROM BELOW ➤ either rejection of home or feelings of an unattainable desirable home situation

FROM ABOVE ➤ rejection of home situation

Placement

BASED ON BOTTOM OF THE PAPER

➤ insecure

➤ no one to rely on

SMALL, HIGH PLACEMENT

➤ tendency to withdraw

➤ fear and avoidance of others

➤ home situation too difficult for artist to handle

ANGLE (15 DEGREES OR MORE)

➤ insecurity

Baseline (the Line the House is On)

OMISSION ➤ lack of solid foundation

➤ in the air

Chimney

Symbol of warm, intimate relations, sometimes associated with phallic symbol. Reinforcement, absence, and size are all important.

OMISSION ➤ lacking psychological warmth

➤ conflicts with significant male figures

➤ longs for nurturing

OVERLY LARGE

➤ overemphasis on sexual concerns and/or possible exhibitionist tendencies

➤ sexual relevance

HEAVY LINE PRESSURE, REINFORCEMENT

➤ sexual relevance

MULTIPLICITY

➤ over-concern about phallus and close relationships

HOUSE

Smoke

Presence, absence, direction, shape, and intensity must be considered.

- ➤ much profusion, swirly, many tightly curved lines, jumbled, chaotic
  - *inner tension*
- ➤ single line
  - *lack of family affection*
- ➤ wispy
  - *little warmth and affection*
- ➤ abundant
  - *warmth and affection within*
- ➤ large smoke trail
  - *sexual relevance*

Door

Represents accessibility.

ABOVE BASELINE, WITHOUT STEPS
- ➤ interpersonal inaccessibility
- ➤ no way to enter

OMISSION
- ➤ extreme difficulty in allowing accessibility to others
- ➤ withdraws from environment by blocking contact
- ➤ no one can enter from the outside

OPEN
- ➤ strong need to receive warmth from external world
- ➤ connotes the potential vulnerability of a person who goes to extreme levels to satisfy this craving

VERY LARGE ➤ overly dependent on others

SMALL DOOR ➤ lack of trust and reluctance to allow access to self

WITH LOCK OR HINGES
- ➤ defensiveness

SIDE OF THE HOUSE
- ➤ withdrawn, inaccessible

Fence

AROUND HOUSE
- ➤ need for emotional protection
- ➤ withdrawal, inaccessibility

Gutters

➤ suspiciousness

Roof

Signifies thinking and fantasy, relative size compared to rest of the house tends to indicate the amount of time spent in fantasy.

UNIDIMENSIONAL (SINGLE LINE CONNECTING TWO WALLS)

➤ unimaginative or emotionally constricted

OVERLY LARGE

➤ seeks satisfaction in fantasy

OVEREMPHASIS

➤ fear of losing control over fantasy life

SMALL ➤ feels stupid, not bright

OMISSION ➤ inability to daydream, to fantasize, or use fantasy appropriately

INCORRECT OR ILLOGICAL PERSPECTIVES

➤ breakdown in logical thinking

Shutters

CLOSED ➤ extreme defensiveness and withdrawal

OPEN ➤ ability to make sensitive interpersonal adjustment

Walkway

VERY LONG ➤ lessened accessibility

NARROW AT HOUSE, BROAD AT END

➤ superficially friendly

Walls

Connote ego strength.

STRONG WALLS

➤ sturdy ego

THIN WALLS ➤ fragile ego

OVEREMPHASIZED WALLS

➤ strong and conscious need for ego control

HOUSE

Window(s)

Personal accessibility, location, adequacy of number and size, proportions, emphasis, and details need to be considered.

OMISSION
- hostile or withdrawing
- won't let anyone see in
- isolated and withdraws from interpersonal contact (sexual relevance)

PRESENT ON GROUND, ABSENT FROM UPPER STORY
- gap between reality and fantasy

ALL ABOVE GROUND LEVEL OR SHADED IN GROUND LEVEL
- secrets

WITH CURTAINS
- reserved, controlled

SHADED OR COVERED BY CURTAINS
- hide and cover over "things" within
- withdrawn, inaccessible

BARE
- behavior is mostly blunt and direct

DISSIMILARITY AND PRESENCE OF A WEDGE-SHAPED WINDOW
- history of sexual abuse

LARGE OPEN WINDOWS
- focusing attention on subject/object in house
- sexual relevance

SMALL
- inaccessible, withdrawn

BARRED, SHUTTERED
- withdrawal, guarded accessibility

Tree

Tree drawings reveal what is within. They project the deepest and most primitive levels of personality and symbolize the reflected hidden feelings about the self. The tree drawing can express the artist's feelings about herself in relationships and relatedness. (Hammer, 1980)

The tree's essential parts are: *roots, trunk, branches, and crown.* By age seven, a child should be able to draw a tree with a trunk and at least one branch. Trees drawn by children after age seven are less subject to developmental variations. (Buck, 1981; Koch, 1952)

Tree (Whole)

EXTREMELY LARGE TREE
> ➤ aggressive tendencies
>
> ➤ fantasy or hypersensitivity

TINY TREE   ➤ inferior, feelings of insignificance

FAINT LINES   ➤ feelings of inadequacy, indecisiveness

TREE COMPOSED OF JUST TWO LINES FOR TRUNK AND LOOPED CROWN
> ➤ impulsive, variable

SHADING, EXCESSIVELY DARK OR REINFORCED
> ➤ hostile defenses or aggressive behaviors

FINE BROKEN LINES
> ➤ overt anxiety

FRUIT TREES AFTER AGE SEVEN
> ➤ excessive abundance of fruit
>   • *dependency needs consuming self*

DISSIMILARITY IN DRAWING STYLES
> ➤ trunk two-dimensional and branches one-dimensional
>   • *good early development interrupted by later trauma*

EXCESSIVE USE OF DETAILS
> ➤ perception of dangerous world
>
> ➤ struggling to maintain ego control

UNRECOGNIZABLE TREES
> ➤ frequently drawn by sexually molested children

PLACEMENT ON BOTTOM EDGE OF PAPER AFTER AGE TEN
> ➤ sign of immaturity

TREE

Type of Tree

FRUIT TREE ➤ drawn by someone over seven depicts possible immaturity (although normal between ages five and seven)

CHRISTMAS TREE
➤ dependency needs

DEAD TREES ➤ depression with profound feelings of inferiority and potential suicidal behavior

PALM TREES ➤ sexual relevance

Placement

RIGHT SIDE ➤ male, father dominance
➤ controlled tendencies, seeks intellectual satisfaction

LEFT SIDE ➤ female, mother dominance
➤ impulsive, emotional, self-centered

TOP ➤ future

MIDDLE ➤ present

LOWER ➤ past

Branches

Branches extend into the environment, so their number, size, dimensions, and the extent of their structure are a metaphor for the personality organization. A well-organized branch structure with well-formed branches represents normal flexibility and satisfactory adjustment.

BARE BRANCHES, ONE-DIMENSIONAL AND FAN-SHAPED
➤ impulsiveness, arrogance, instability

FALLING ➤ possibility of losing ability to cope with pressures

DEAD ➤ traumatic experience
➤ loss of capacity to receive interpersonal satisfaction

BROKEN ➤ associated with trauma, e.g., accident, illness, rape
➤ sexual relevance

OVERLY LARGE BRANCH STRUCTURE
➤ concern with having needs met by others

BRANCHES DIRECTED TOWARDS CENTER OF THE TREE OR ARCHED INWARD
> ➤ sense of independence and possible withdrawal from others

Crown, Leaves

Crown and branch structure is associated with the ability (intellectual and social) to interact and derive satisfaction from the environment.

ENCLOSED
> ➤ encapsulating
> ➤ outside forces cannot reach in
> ➤ prohibits self from reaching out

SPACE BETWEEN CROWN AND TRUNK
> ➤ feelings and mental processes are disconnected
> ➤ inability to self-care

CROWN FALLING DOWN ONTO AND OVER THE TRUNK
> ➤ individuals have nothing within
> ➤ driven by others

SCRIBBLED, DISORGANIZED CROWN
> ➤ impulsiveness
> ➤ confused thinking and value structure

CUT OFF AT TOP
> ➤ social isolation

EXAGGERATED EMPHASIS ON THE CROWN
> ➤ inhibited emotionally
> ➤ analytical

LOOPED CROWN
> ➤ impulsive, variable

Trunk

Embodies feelings of basic power, ego intactness, and inner strength.

HEAVILY SHADED
> ➤ anxiety

EXAGGERATED EMPHASIS ON THE TRUNK
> ➤ emotional immaturity

DASHED LINE IN OUTLINE OF TRUNK
> ➤ anxiety, impulsiveness, instability

TREE

LIGHTLY SKETCHED SIDES OF TRUNK

➤ feelings of impending ego breakdown

SCARS, HOLES, KNOTHOLES

➤ feelings of damage

➤ associated with trauma, e.g., accident, illness, rape

➤ trauma placement: relative age (closest to crown being current age)

➤ circles inside: trauma experienced in past and healing

➤ blackened: shame associated with experience

➤ large: preoccupation with procreation

➤ small animal inside: ambivalence surrounding child-bearing

KNOTHOLES ➤ sexual symbolism

• *diamond-shaped or small; related to vagina*

• *small and simple; sexual assault or initial sexual experience*

• *outline reinforced; shock impact greater*

BROAD TRUNK

➤ dominant emotional life

THIN TRUNK

➤ tenuous sense of inner strength and power

TRUNCATED ➤ developing ego functions curtailed

Roots

Symbolic indices of personality stability, secure grounding, and instinctual life.

THIN AND TRANSPARENT

➤ tenuous grasp of reality, flimsy hold

EXAGGERATED EMPHASIS ON ROOTS

➤ emotional responses shallow

➤ reasoning limited

NO ROOTS, NO GROUND LINE PRESENT

➤ repressed emotions

➤ lack of connection to the environment

Frequently Drawn Miscellaneous Details

Other miscellaneous details frequently found in children's drawings are listed below. These provide additional information that complements the analysis of the drawings of the person, house, and tree.

Adornment
JEWELRY, HAIR CLIPS, BOWS, DETAILED CLOTHING SUGGESTING
MATURE FEMININITY
> ➤ sexual relevance

Age Representation
MATURE, OLDER-LOOKING THAN THE ARTIST
> ➤ sexual relevance

IMMATURE, YOUNGER THAN THE ARTIST
> ➤ powerless, helpless
> ➤ sexual relevance

Barriers
FENCES, GATES, PROHIBITING, LIMITING VIEW, OBJECTS MAKING IT VISUALLY
HARDER TO SEE THE PERSON, HOUSE, OR TREE
> ➤ lack of trust, suspicious, alert for danger

Beds, Bedroom
> ➤ sexualization or depression

Belts
WIDE, LOW   ➤ inner struggle to maintain control over sexual drives
> ➤ sexual preoccupation

Birds
> ➤ wish to flee from stress and pressure in the environment

Buttons
> ➤ connotes strong dependency needs

Cartoon Figures
> ➤ withdrawn, inaccessible

Chimney Smoke
ABSENCE   ➤ no warmth

HEAVY, SCRIBBLED

> ➤ anxiety, tension

LARGE SMOKE TRAIL

> ➤ sexual relevance

Circles

EXTRANEOUS CIRCLES

> ➤ suggestive of sexual abuse

Clothes

UNDERCLOTHES, LACK OF SPECIFIC PIECES OF CLOTHING, E.G., SHIRT, LONG TROUSERS

> ➤ sexual relevance

BATHING SUIT, MUCH BODY EXPOSURE

> ➤ sexual relevance

OVERSIZED—COVER UP

> ➤ cover ugliness, body drives, low self-esteem

Clouds

SHADED, SWIRLY, CHAOTIC

> ➤ anxiety and depression

PLACEMENT OVER DRAWN IMAGES

> ➤ anxiety over self, home environment shadows the image

MULTIPLE CLOUDS

> ➤ flooding of inner tensions

Clowns

> ➤ concealment device among severely traumatized female sexual victims
> ➤ feelings of shame

Cosmetic Emphasis

> ➤ sexual relevance

Door

PEEPHOLES ➤ suspicious, lack of trust, alert for danger

LOCKED, HEAVILY HINGED

> ➤ suspicious, lack of trust

Doorknobs

SHADED   ➤ concern about connection with others

ABSENCE   ➤ others cannot get in

HIGH PLACEMENT ON THE DOOR
    ➤ difficult to get in

Dress

OVERSIZED   ➤ feels inadequate, can't fill up the dress

Food

ABSENCE ON DINNER TABLE
    ➤ no nurturing

Grass

SPIKY, SHARP, POINTED
    ➤ hostility, anger

Ground Line

NOT CONNECTED TO DRAWN IMAGES
    ➤ insecurity, wish to stabilize environment

Monsters

    ➤ internalized monster

    ➤ inner tensions too strong, unable to use ego resources for constructive solutions

Poisonous Plants

    ➤ sees self as venomous

Rain

    ➤ tears, sad

Scars

FACE, BODY   ➤ sexual relevance

Shoes

ELABORATION, E.G., LACES, DECORATIONS
    ➤ emphasis on sexual impulse is present

SYMBOLIC OF PHALLUS AND SEXUALITY

Ties

DRAWN BY MALES

> ➤ sexual relevance

These are the most frequent characteristics found in drawings of the person, house, and tree. When looking at drawings, it is easy to focus on the characteristic that stands out most. The checklist will help you identify other characteristics that might be overlooked. It is helpful to look at the drawings at different times because your perspective will change with your different moods, thoughts, and feelings. With each fresh viewing, you may find additional significant characteristics previously overlooked, or disregard marginal characteristics.

The drawings represent the child's feelings, and all should consistently provide information that supports the main message the child is sending. There should be enough drawings to substantiate that the child's feelings represent her general condition rather than her feelings on a particular day. A child with low self-esteem will show her low self-esteem in her drawing in various ways, whether she is experiencing an angry or happy day.

W O R K B O O K

All the pictures in this section were drawn by emotionally, physically, and sexually abused children. First is a series of six drawings by a seven-year-old girl. These drawings represent how the artist continues to represent distress over a period of time. They also demonstrate consistency in symbolic meanings of the characteristics presented.

The subsequent drawings are examples of characteristics. A list of the significant characteristics that relate to each drawing accompanies each one. The age and sex of the artist, the presenting problem, and the global impression are included.

Drawings 1 through 15 in the Reader's Practice Section include only information about the age and sex of the artist. You may use these drawings to practice identifying inherent characteristics. At the end of this section is a list of characteristics for each drawing so you can check your observations. The global or first impressions for these drawings are subjective and yours may differ from the author's.

However, your identification of the characteristics will be objective and should agree with those listed. These will either support or negate your first impression. Recognizing the characteristics and their meanings is a straightforward process.

When I look at a drawing I usually note the characteristic that first attracts my attention. Then I use the checklist of steps in "Analyzing Drawings," and Chapter 4, "Characteristics," for the interpretations.

All the drawings are a result of three instructions:

1) *Draw a picture of yourself.*
2) *Draw a picture of a house (or house and tree).*
3) *Draw a picture of a tree.*

Some drawings are composed of more than what was requested. I have included them to illustrate the artist sending signals by giving us additional information. Rather than being rigid and insisting that a child draws exactly what you request, it is important to stay open and understand what the child wants us to know.

Series of Six Drawings

These are examples of a series of pictures drawn by a seven-year-old girl. They are primarily drawings of herself, showing subtle changes over a period of three months. The pictures and the portrayed characteristics differ, but the same theme in symbolic meaning repeats itself. The girl was brought in for treatment because she had become extremely passive and withdrawn in school and had stopped playing with her classmates. After the three-month evaluation there was enough evidence to indicate emotional, physical, and sexual abuse. The girl's father was removed from the home.

SERIES 1

- ➤ **Hair** – excessive, exaggerated hair
- ➤ **Eyes** – without pupils, different sizes, shaded
- ➤ **Ears** – shaded, one large, one small
- ➤ **Mouth** – large, down-turned
- ➤ **Head** – large
- ➤ **Body** – enlargement, shaded area
- ➤ **Arms and hands** – omission (often drawn by sexually abused children)
- ➤ **Legs** – single thin line

SERIES 2

➤ **Head** – very large

➤ **Eyes** – tiny

➤ **Ears** – omission

➤ **Mouth** – down-turned

➤ **Body** – weird shape, shaded area

➤ **Arm and hands** – omission

➤ **Legs** – single thin line

➤ **Tree** – floating, middle of page

➤ **Trunk** – shaded, triangular-shaped with point on bottom (not stable)

➤ **Branch system** – enclosed (holding self together)

➤ **Leaves** – enclosed

➤ **Roots** – omission

➤ **Houses** – two disproportionately small houses, no ground line, shaded

➤ **Doors** – one door above baseline, no door in the other

➤ **Roof** – one small roof, one large roof

➤ **Windows** – above ground level, dissimilar, wedge-shaped

➤ **Details** – shaded sky, clouds, shaded bird, tears on face

SERIES 3

- ➤ **Head** – very large
- ➤ **Hair** – messy
- ➤ **Body** – drawn like a four-year-old, shaded, big circle around small shaded circle (placement in genital area), open trunk
- ➤ **Arms and hands** – omission
- ➤ **Legs** – single thin line, not touching ground line
- ➤ **Feet** – omission
- ➤ **Circles** – extraneous (on face and body)
- ➤ **Tree** – floating, at an angle
- ➤ **Trunk** – heavily shaded
- ➤ **Leaves** – enclosed
- ➤ **Roots** – omission
- ➤ **Details** – shaded clouds
- ➤ **Adornment** – earrings
- ➤ **Clouds**

SERIES 4

- ➤ **Head** – very large
- ➤ **Eyes** – without pupils
- ➤ **Mouth** – large
- ➤ **Face** – shaded
- ➤ **Hair** – excessive, exaggerated
- ➤ **Arms and hands** – omission
- ➤ **Body** – shaded
- ➤ **Adornments** – earrings, small necklace, large shaded necklace with jewel covering her genital area
- ➤ **Shoes** – tiptoes, pointed, different size
- ➤ **Tree** – floating
- ➤ **Trunk** – shaded, pointed bottom (unstable)
- ➤ **Roots** – omission
- ➤ **Leaves** – enclosed
- ➤ **Details** – shaded sky, shaded black clouds, lots of birds

SERIES 5

➤ **Tree** – small, no ground line

➤ **Roots** – omission

➤ **Leaves** – scribbled, disorganized crown, exaggerated emphasis on the crown, chaotic

➤ **Details** – chaotic, large shaded lightning bolts striking the tree, big tidal wave with shaded foam

➤ **Sky** – Scribbled, shaded, completely covering three-fourths of the picture

SERIES 6

Beginning of some changes in structural organization

- ➤ **Head** – large
- ➤ **Hair** – messy
- ➤ **Eyes** – no pupils
- ➤ **Body** – shaded, small, boxlike
- ➤ **Arms** – outward-reaching, shaded
- ➤ **Hands** – mittenlike
- ➤ **Fingers** – spike-like
- ➤ **Legs** – long, shaded
- ➤ **Details** – cloud, bird, tall grass
- ➤ **Eyelashes** – exaggerated
- ➤ **Sky** – heavily shaded directly above her

Global Impression

An invitation, a smiling, mature young girl with open arms.

SPECIFIC CHARACTERISTICS

➤ **Arms** – outward-reaching, (reaching out for contact)

➤ **Hair** – long, excessive, shaded (anxiety, impulses breaking through, physical abuse, sexual abuse)

➤ **Head** – very large, over one-fourth size of body (sexual, physical abuse)

➤ **Eyelashes** – distinctive (femininity important)

➤ **Mouth** – large (orally erotic)

➤ **Lips** – Cupid's bow (sexual relevance)

➤ **Face** – mask-like (emotional numbing, hidden feelings)

➤ **Body** – heavily shaded (anxiety, sexual relevance)

➤ **Maturity** – age representation older (sexual relevance)

➤ **Adornments** – earrings (sexual relevance)

➤ **Feet** – omission (helplessness, cannot control environment, can't move)

TRAUMA

Molested by her stepfather when she was six.

Global Impression

Silly, crazy-looking person.

SPECIFIC CHARACTERISTICS

➤ **Head** – extremely large (sexual, physical abuse)

➤ **Arms** – outward-reaching (desire for contact), short (ineptitude in reaching others)

➤ **Hands** – absence of well-defined hands ("take care of me," sexual relevance)

➤ **Open trunk** – no closure between legs (open and vulnerable, empty of feelings, powerless, sexual relevance)

➤ **Eyes** – tiny, without pupils (possible sexual abuse)

➤ **Face** – shaded (seriously disturbed, poor self-concept)

➤ **Mouth** – very large (orally erotic)

➤ **Teeth** – fang-like (aggressive, hostility)

➤ **Hair** – tightly curled (anxiety about own thoughts)

➤ **Legs** – single line (powerlessness, vulnerability)

➤ **Feet** – omission (helplessness, cannot walk)

➤ **Shading** – chest region and genital area (concern, anxiety, sexual relevance)

➤ **Clouds** – hanging over her (anxiety directly over her)

➤ **Adornment** – earrings (sexual relevance)

TRAUMA

Sexually abused by her father from age two to age four.

Global Impression

Disturbing appearance of people. Picture of self became four different people. Smallest figure is least developed. It appears she is placing her separate feelings into these different people.

SPECIFIC CHARACTERISTICS

- ➤ **Developmental discrepancy** – (draws like a four-year-old)
- ➤ **Arms** – omission in three figures (inability to control environment, strong need to regulate impulses, inadequate, helpless, passive, guilt over hostility or sexuality, sexual relevance) arms drawn on one figure like a four-year-old, (possible arrested development at that age)
- ➤ **Body** – missing in three figures (denial of body drives and feelings)
- ➤ **Mouth** – overly emphasized, large (immaturity, oral aggressive, orally erotic)
- ➤ **Nose** – on two figures large and heavily outlined (sexual relevance)
- ➤ **Teeth** – sharp, pointed, exposed (aggressive acting out, anger)
- ➤ **Nose** – large, heavily outlined (sexual relevance)
- ➤ **Shading** – body (sexual relevance), face (low self-concept, seriously disturbed)
- ➤ **Feet** – omission (helplessness, unable to walk, not connected to the ground)
- ➤ **Hands** – omission (not able to connect)
- ➤ **Eyes** – large, wide open (suspicious, lack of trust, alert to danger)
- ➤ **Clouds** – shaded and hanging over head (feeling great anxiety)
- ➤ **Adornment** – earrings (sexual relevance)

TRAUMA

Sexually abused by her father when she was four.

Global Impression

Chaos.

SPECIFIC CHARACTERISTICS

➤ **Large house** – (aggression, hostility, overcompensates)

➤ **Ground line** – omission (in the air)

➤ **Door** – scribbled heavy strokes and shaded (anxiety about letting anyone in), above baseline (interpersonal inaccessibility, no way to enter)

➤ **Window** – large, barred, shaded, second floor, (secrets, hide and cover over "things" within, withdrawn, inaccessible)

➤ **Chimney** – overly large (overemphasis on sexual concerns and/or possible exhibitionist tendencies, sexual relevance)

➤ **Smoke** – large smoke trail, swirly (inner tension, sexual relevance)

➤ **Tree** – apple (dependency)

➤ **Trunk** – dashed line in outline and within trunk, lightly sketched (anxiety, impulsivity, instability, feelings of impending ego breakdown)

➤ **Tree crown** – encapsulated (holding her anxieties in), falling down onto and over the trunk (nothing within, driven by others)

➤ **Knothole** – large, lightly shaded (feelings of damage, trauma), placement approximately one-fourth from the bottom (trauma around the age of two)

➤ **Roots** – omission (repressed emotions)

➤ **Second tree** – no trunk (no feelings of power, ego intactness, inner strength)

➤ **Crown** – scribbled, disorganized crown (impulsiveness, confused thinking and value structure)

➤ **Clouds** – shaded (anxiety overhead)

➤ **Details** – decoration on side of the house, flags, huge sun with a face, and a rainbow over the house (wanting structure)

TRAUMA

Sexually molested by her father who had access to her until she was two.

The Artist   Girl, age seven and one-half

Global Impression

Disturbing, a dark heavy feeling even though she and two trees are floating, an angry tension.

SPECIFIC CHARACTERISTICS

➤ **Placement** – upper half of the paper, floating in air (striving toward unrealistic goals or expectations), one tree on ground line, not rooted (feelings of insecurity, repressed emotions)

➤ **Shading** – very heavy shading (much anxiety, agitation)

➤ **Lines** – heavy, reinforced (inner tension, aggressive, hostile, forcefulness)

➤ **Tree** – apple tree (dependency and immaturity)

➤ **Branches** – bare (impulsiveness, arrogance, instability), overly large branch structure (concern with needs being met)

➤ **Crown** – enclosed (outside forces can't reach in, prohibits self from reaching out)

➤ **Trunk** – exaggerated emphasis (emotional immaturity), heavily shaded (anxiety), scars, knotholes (feelings of damage, trauma), blackened (shame associated with experience), placement – middle (trauma at four years), broad (dominant emotional life)

➤ **Person** – heavy shading (lots of anxiety)

➤ **Genital Area** – heavily shaded circle over genital area (area of conflict, sexual relevance)

➤ **Arms** – outward (desire for contact), different size (suggestive of sexual abuse), heavily shaded (guilt regarding sexual impulses, aggressive impulses)

➤ **Hands** – big hands and large fingers (acting out behavior, anger)

➤ **Body** – shaded (sexual relevance, angry, aggressive, hostile)

➤ **Face** – shaded (seriously disturbed, poor self-concept)

➤ **Eyes** – without pupils (sexual relevance)

➤ **Nose** – shaded (sexual relevance)

➤ **Mouth** – large (orally erotic)

➤ **Legs** – thin line (powerlessness, vulnerability)

➤ **Hair** – shaded (anxiety, impulse breaking through)

➤ **Adornment** – extremely large hair bow (sexual relevance)

TRAUMA

Sexually molested by an uncle between ages four and six.

Reader's Practice Section

This section gives you the chance to practice the systematic approach outlined in this guide. It includes fifteen pictures drawn by abused children. Each drawing contains various characteristics signifying trauma. Obviously, not all the listed characteristics will be represented in these drawings, but you will get an idea of how to identify important characteristics.

Use the following steps to begin this practice. Once you feel comfortable with the process, you will probably develop your own approach which will include these steps:

1) Record your first impression and/or the global impression.

2) List the characteristics that stand out. Look them up in Chapter 4, "Characteristics," and jot down the interpretations.

3) Go through the checklist in "Analyzing Drawings" and list all the missed characteristics that show signs of distress along with their interpretations.

4) Verify your observations with characteristics that are listed for each drawing in the back of this section.

When you work with your own drawings, it helps to record your observations on a piece of paper and attach it to the picture. When you review a series of drawings you will then have all the observations close at hand without having to repeat the same procedure.

The Artist   Girl, age seven and one-half

welcome

Checklist of Characteristics
for Drawings 1–15

1	PERSON	**2**	PERSON

1 PERSON

The Artist   Girl, age seven

2 PERSON

The Artist   Girl, age eight

✓ **Size** – small

✓ **Hair** – exaggerated

✓ **Face** – shaded

✓ **Eyes** – no pupils

✓ **Mouth** – very large

✓ **Arms** – different size

✓ **Hands** – very large

✓ **Body** – shaded, angle

✓ **Legs** – transparent, wide stance

✓ **Ground line** – not connected

✓ **Details** – shoes, very large and shaded,
  eyelashes exaggerated

TRAUMA

Sexually molested by house painter.

✓ **Eyes** – without pupils, small

✓ **Mouth** – large

✓ **Hair** – thinning at crown, long at sides

✓ **Neck** – thick, elongated

✓ **Body** – shaded

✓ **Transparency** – legs seen through pants

✓ **Legs** – single thin line

✓ **Arms** – large, differential treatment, outward
  reaching

✓ **Hands** – mittenlike

✓ **Fingers** – spikes

✓ **Ground** – spiky grass

✓ **Cloud** – large with raindrops

✓ **Umbrella** – in hand but not covering her,
  unable to take care of herself

TRAUMA

Father abused her physically and possibly
molested her sexually.

3 PERSON
The Artist Boy, age eight

✓ **Head only**

✓ **Hair** – spiky

✓ **Ears** – large

✓ **Eyes** – extremely small, behind glasses,
no pupils

✓ **Nose** – large

✓ **Nostrils** – emphasized

✓ **Mouth** – open and large

✓ **Tooth** – exposed

✓ **Beard** – spiky

TRAUMA
Sexually abused by a neighbor. Parents were recovering from addiction problems and were not available to protect the child.

4 PERSON
The Artist Girl, age nine

✓ **Head** – very large

✓ **Mouth** – large

✓ **Eyes** – wide open, detailed with eyelashes

✓ **Teeth** – exposed

✓ **Face** – shaded

✓ **Body** – stick figure under triangular body

✓ **Fingers** – spiky

✓ **Hair** – thin on top, long on sides, messy

✓ **Grass** – spiky, pointed

✓ **Legs** – single line

✓ **Feet** – omission

✓ **Clouds** – multiple

✓ **Sky** – shaded, lightning bolts

TRAUMA
Sexually molested by her father from ages three to six. She exhibited aggressive behavior and was out of control in the classroom.

5 PERSON

The Artist Girl, age seven

✓ **Hair** – exaggerated, messy, abundant

✓ **Face** – shaded

✓ **Eyes** – no pupils

✓ **Mouth** – large

✓ **Neck** – wide and elongated, not connected to head

✓ **Body** – shaded

✓ **Arms** – differential treatment

✓ **Hands** – omission

✓ **Legs** – size difference, wide stance

✓ **Feet** – omission

✓ **Clouds** – large, chaotic, messy shading around clouds

TRAUMA

Sexually and physically abused by her father when she was five.

6 PERSON

The Artist Girl, age eight

✓ **Age discrepancy** – representation much older than artist's years

✓ **Head** – very large

✓ **Mouth** – large

✓ **Lips** – Cupid's bow

✓ **Hair** – exaggerated, long on sides, abundant

✓ **Neck** – thin and elongated

✓ **Arms** – long, different size, outward-reaching

✓ **Legs** – shaded

✓ **Body** – shaded

✓ **No ground line**

✓ **Feet** – different sizes, one foot very large

✓ **Details** – heavily shaded flowers on dress covering genital area, eyelashes

✓ **Adornment** – ring

TRAUMA

Molested by her stepfather when she was six.

✓ **Eyes** – no pupils

✓ **Mouth** – large

✓ **Lips** – Cupid's bow

✓ **Ears** – conspicuous, shaded

✓ **Hands** – absence of well-defined hands

✓ **Fingers** – on right hand, not on left

✓ **Breasts** – two nipples drawn

✓ **Stomach** – blackened circle

✓ **Genitals**

✓ **Feet** – large

✓ **Body**– scars

TRAUMA

Sexually abused by an older neighbor bully.

✓ **Placement** – appears to be in the air in a sleeping-bag, cannot tell if she is outside or inside the house

✓ **Shading** – chaotic scribbles

✓ **Eyes** – without pupils

✓ **Body** – stick figure, minimalist

✓ **Transparency** – Can see the body in the sleeping bag, unable to determine if she is in the house or outside; she is lying on the grass but the windows in the house are seen from the inside; confusing

✓ **Grass** – not connected to the ground

✓ **Windows** – shaded, heavily curtained

✓ **Door** – omission

✓ **House** – incomplete

✓ **Ground** – house disconnected from ground

✓ **Walls** – thick

✓ **Sky** – chaotic, shaded scribbles

TRAUMA

Sexually molested by the gardener when she was five.

✓ **House** – incomplete

✓ **Chimney** – omission

✓ **Door** – omission

✓ **Size** – house very large

✓ **Roof** – large

✓ **Windows** – above ground floor, barred, dissimilarity of windows with the attic window wedge-shaped

✓ **Clouds and ground** – heavily shaded

✓ **Details** – excessive flowers, large and shaded, chaotic shading, forms a barrier

TRAUMA

Sexual abuse by day-school aide suspected when she was four.

✓ **Placement** – bottom of paper

✓ **Large**

✓ **Shading** – basic house, door (hardly noticeable), tree, sun over the tree

✓ **Windows** – curtains, barred, dissimilarity

✓ **Roof** – very large, illogical perspective

✓ **Chimney** – overly large, no smoke

✓ **Door** – on baseline, not clearly defined, doorknob half on door and half on front wall

✓ **Tree** – shaped like a Christmas tree

✓ **Trunk** – not on ground, no roots

✓ **Crown** – reinforced lines

✓ **Gutters**

✓ **Person** – enclosed in a box on top of the sun

TRAUMA

Physically and emotionally abused by drug-addicted parents.

98

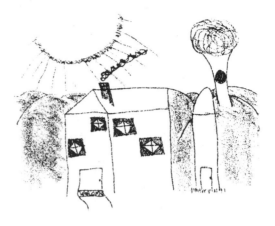

✓ **Age discrepancy** – immature

✓ **House** – incomplete

✓ **Baseline** – omission

✓ **Roof** – shaded

✓ **Door** – large, decoration on door but no doorknob

✓ **Windows** – faint lines

✓ **Trunk** – sturdy and broad, exaggerated emphasis, scars

✓ **Roots** – omission

✓ **Tree** – angle

✓ **Crown** – small and enclosed, shaded

TRAUMA

Sexually abused by stepfather from ages three to five.

✓ **Windows** – barred and curtained, all above ground floor

✓ **Chimney** – shaded

✓ **Baseline** – omission

✓ **Door** – above baseline without steps

✓ **Small house** – no windows, no chimney, tall and skinny, spiky grass at bottom

✓ **Trunk** – sturdy

✓ **Knothole** – large, heavily shaded, placement middle of the trunk (trauma at six years)

✓ **Crown** – enclosed, chaotic

✓ **Roots** – omission

✓ **Hills** – shaded

TRAUMA

Sexually abused by successive men from ages two to six, when she was adopted. Lived in a series of foster homes after eight months of age. Mother and father are both unknown to her.

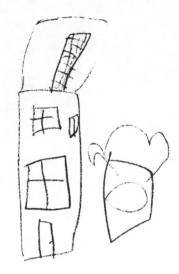

✓ **Very large house**

✓ **Windows** – all above ground level, barred, dissimilarity

✓ **Chimney** – overly large

✓ **Roof** – incorrect, illogical perspective

✓ **Tree** – base in an angle, precarious balance

✓ **Crown** – enclosed, simple loop

✓ **Trunk** – very broad, large knothole

✓ **Roots** – omission

✓ **No ground line**

✓ **Doorknob** – omission

TRAUMA

Possible sexual abuse by drug-addicted mother.

✓ **Shaded** – tree, person

✓ **Trunk** – knothole heavily shaded, placement three-fourths up from the bottom (trauma at seven)

✓ **Angle**

✓ **Apple tree**

✓ **Crown** – scribbled and disorganized

✓ **Branch system** – large

✓ **Roots** – exaggerated

✓ **Grass or bushes around the tree trunk** – shaded, spiky

✓ **Hair** – shaded, excessive, exaggerated

✓ **Face** – no features

✓ **Arms** – heavily shaded, long, differential treatment

✓ **Hands** – very large, spiky fingers

✓ **Neck** – wide and elongated

✓ **Body** – shaded

✓ **Pants** – heavily shaded

✓ **Bird** – very large, shaded wings and tail

✓ **Clouds**

✓ **Sky** – shaded, scribbled

✓ **Details** – shoes and shoelaces

TRAUMA

Sexually abused by mother's boyfriend when she was seven years old.

The Artist   Girl, age seven

- ✓ **Age discrepancy** – immature
- ✓ **Branches** – overly large
- ✓ **Crown** – scribbled, chaotic
- ✓ **No ground line**
- ✓ **Roots** – omission
- ✓ **Whole tree** – composed of two lines for the trunk with large branches as a crown, almost unrecognizable
- ✓ **Trunk** – two lines flaring out

TRAUMA

Seven-year-old girl abandoned by mother.

CONCLUSION

The main goal of this book is to enable you to gather enough information to decide whether or not a child should be evaluated by experts. But how much information do you need to collect before making a decision?

This is really your judgment call. If the child's behavior, personal history, environmental situation, and drawings are all alarming, you obviously do not need to collect drawings over an extended period of time. However, if the drawn characteristics suggest abuse, but the behavior is not alarming, it is essential to analyze many drawings over a period of time to determine if a constant pattern of distress exists. A consistent pattern of characteristics that suggest abuse must appear.

When abuse or trauma exist in a child's life, each drawing will usually have a multitude of characteristics suggesting abuse or sexual relevance. *A single characteristic is not enough to indicate abuse.* The characteristics that suggest abuse should appear consistently in a series. For example, if an alarming picture is followed by another picture with a happy theme, the "happy" drawing should also have characteristics designating abuse. The theme or subject matter will not hide the characteristics that indicate abuse. Relevant characteristics must also support each other. For example, if a drawing contains two characteristics that may indicate sexual abuse (e.g., a very large head with vacant eyes and thin hair on top), you still need to find other signs supporting the hypothesis of sexual abuse. These include characteristics of sexual relevance, insecurity, anger, low self esteem, etc. Over a period of time the characteristics representing the different feelings of trauma will continue appearing in the drawings. When you

have gathered enough information to feel confident that a pattern exists, you can recommend that an expert evaluate the child.

When analyzing drawings, you must also beware of over-interpreting characteristics. The subject of children at risk is highly emotional, and it is easy to jump to conclusions. *You must be extra careful not to attribute more meaning to the drawings than is actually there.* If houses, trees, hills, or other objects have a phallic or breast shape, for example, we can be tempted to single out these characteristics and ignore everything else. This makes the analysis totally subjective, with greatly increased chances for misinterpretation.

We therefore must make every attempt to remove subjective elements from the analyzing process. Following the objective, systematic approach to art analysis presented in this guide will help you achieve this. The characteristics and interpretations published by expert art therapists have already been widely accepted in academic and professional circles. They give you a concrete, unbiased foundation on which to base your analysis. The Appendix lists the major works of experts in the art therapy field by characteristics. If you are interested in further details on interpreting children's drawings, you should refer to these books. The checklists will also help you focus on all the relevant characteristics that collectively signify trauma.

Do not interrogate the child. If you suspect abuse, it is wise to have an expert do the evaluation so that the child is not further traumatized. Inappropriate questioning has contaminated many cases. We must all remember that our emotions can be relayed to a child and can often confuse the issue.

If you have colleagues, it is extremely helpful to work in collaboration. An extra point of view adds to the information pool, especially when people with different perspectives work together. This process will encourage objectivity.

The goal is to help bring children out of their distress before pathology becomes their way of life. The process of viewing a drawing in a systematic way is a tool we can all use to help identify a child who is potentially at risk.

REFERENCE LIST OF MAJOR CHARACTERISTICS
Appendix

General

Details (Di Leo, 1983; Hammer, 1980; Jolles, 1971; Kaufman and Wohl, 1992; Klepsch and Logie, 1982; Ogdon, 1977; Oster and Gould 1987; Van Hutton, 1994; Wohl and Kaufman, 1985)

Erasures (Di Leo, 1983; Hammer, 1980; Kaufman and Wohl, 1992; Koppitz, 1968; Machover, 1980; Oster and Gould, 1987)

Lines (Di Leo, 1983; Kaufman and Wohl, 1992; Klepsch and Logie, 1982; Oster and Gould, 1987; Van Hutton, 1994; Wohl and Kaufman, 1985)

Placement (Bolander, 1977; Buck, 1973; Di Leo, 1983; Hammer, 1980; Kaufman and Wohl, 1992; Koppitz, 1968; Machover, 1980)

Pressure (Di Leo, 1983; Hammer, 1980; Kaufman and Wohl, 1992; Ogdon, 1977)

Shading (Di Leo, 1983; Hammer, 1980; Jolles, 1971; Kaufman and Wohl, 1992; Kelley, 1984; Klepsch and Logie, 1982; Ogdon, 1977; Oster and Gould, 1987; Van Hutton, 1994; Wohl and Kaufman, 1985)

Transparencies (Di Leo, 1983; Kaufman and Wohl, 1992; Machover, 1980; Ogdon, 1977; Oster and Gould, 1987; Van Hutton, 1994; Wohl and Kaufman, 1985)

Person

Person (Whole) (Buck, 1973, 1981; Di Leo, 1973; Handler and Reyher, 1964; Jolles, 1971; Kaufman and Wohl, 1992; Kelley, 1984; Klepsch and Logie, 1982; Koppitz, 1968; Machover, 1949, 1980; Ogdon, 1977; Oster and Gould, 1987; Van Hutton, 1994; Wohl and Kaufman, 1985)

Arms (Buck, 1966; Di Leo, 1983; Hammer, 1980; Jolles, 1971; Kelley, 1984; Klepsch and Logie 1982; Koppitz, 1968; Machover, 1980; Oster and Gould, 1987; Saarni and Azara, 1977; Van Hutton, 1994; Wohl and Kaufman, 1985)

Beard (Wohl and Kaufman, 1985; Van Hutton, 1994)

Body (Trunk) (Burns, 1983; Burns and Kaufman, 1970; Di Leo, 1983; Kaufman and Wohl, 1992; Koppitz, 1968; Machover, 1949; Malchiodi, 1990; Ogdon, 1977; Oster and Gould, 1987; Van Hutton, 1994; Wohl and Kaufman, 1985)

Breasts (Hibbard et al., 1987; Kelley, 1985; Machover, 1949; Van Hutton, 1994; Wohl and Kaufman, 1985)

Chest (Kaufman and Wohl, 1992)

Ears (Di Leo, 1983; Jolles, 1971; Kaufman and Wohl, 1992; Koppitz, 1968; Machover, 1980; Van Hutton, 1994)

Eyes (Burns and Kaufman, 1972; Di Leo, 1973, 1983; Kaufman and Wohl, 1992; Kelley, 1984; Koppitz, 1968; Machover, 1949; Malchiodi, 1990; Oster and Gould, 1987; Saarni and Azara, 1977; Van Hutton, 1994)

Face (Jolles, 1971; Kaufman and Wohl, 1992; Machover, 1949; Oster and Gould, 1987; Van Hutton, 1994)

Feet (Buck, 1966; Jolles, 1971; Kaufman and Wohl, 1992; Kelley, 1984; Klepsch and Logie,1982; Van Hutton, 1994)

Fingers (Buck, 1948; Hammer 1980; Jolles, 1969; Kaufman and Wohl, 1992; Machover, 1949)

Genitals and Secondary Sexual Features (Di Leo, 1973; Hibbard and Finkelhor, 1987; Kaufman and Wohl, 1992; Kelley, 1984; Klepsch and Logie, 1982; Koppitz, 1968; Machover, 1949, 1980; Van Hutton, 1994)

Hair (Buck, 1948; Jolles, 1971; Kaufman and Wohl, 1992; Koppitz, 1968; Machover, 1980; Ogdon, 1977; Schneidman, 1958; Wohl and Kaufman, 1985; Van Hutton, 1994)

Hands (Buck, 1948, 1966; Burgess et al., 1981; Burns and Kaufman, 1972; Hammer, 1980; Kaufman and Wohl, 1992; Kelley, 1984; Koppitz, 1968; Oster and Gould, 1987; Saarni and Azara, 1977; Van Hutton, 1994; Wohl and Kaufman, 1985)

Head (Blain et al., 1981; Culbertson and Revel, 1987; Jolles, 1971; Kaufman and Wohl, 1992; Machover, 1980; Ogdon, 1977; Van Hutton, 1994)

Legs (Buck, 1948; Hammer, 1954; Jolles, 1969; Kaufman and Wohl, 1992; Koppitz, 1968; Machover, 1949; Van Hutton, 1994)

Lips (Machover, 1949; Van Hutton, 1994)

Mouth (Jolles, 1969; Kaufman and Wohl, 1992; Kelley, 1984; Machover, 1949)

Neck (Buck and Hammer, 1969; Kaufman and Wohl, 1992; Kelley, 1984; Koppitz, 1968; Machover, 1949; Van Hutton, 1992; Wohl and Kaufman, 1985)

Nose (Jolles, 1971; Machover, 1949; Klepsch and Logie, 1982)

Nostrils (Burns and Kaufman, 1972; Machover, 1949)

Pelvic Area (Kelley, 1984)

Shoulders (Buck, 1948; Hammer, 1980; Jolles, 1969; Kaufman and Wohl, 1992; Machover, 1949; Van Hutton, 1994)

Teeth (Buck, 1948; Burns and Kaufman, 1972; Di Leo, 1983; Kaufman and Wohl, 1992; Machover, 1949; Oster and Gould, 1987; Saarni and Azara, 1977; Wohl and Kaufman, 1985)

Waist (Kaufman and Wohl, 1992; Machover, 1980; Van Hutton, 1994)

Sexual

Frequently drawn characteristics by sexually and physically abused children

(Cohen and Phelps, 1985; Culbertson and Revel, 1987; Kelley, 1984; Malchiodi, 1990; Stember, 1978; Van Hutton, 1994)

House

House (Whole) (Buck, 1966, 1948; Hammer, 1980; Kaufman and Wohl, 1992; Koppitz, 1968; Van Hutton, 1994; Wohl and Kaufman, 1985)

Perspective (Oster and Gould, 1987)

Baseline (Jolles, 1971; Kaufman and Wohl, 1992; Klepsch and Logie, 1982; Oster and Gould, 1987)

Chimney (Buck, 1948; Di Leo, 1971; Hammer, 1969; Jolles, 1969; Kaufman and Wohl, 1992; Ogdon, 1977; Oster and Gould, 1987; Van Hutton, 1994; Wohl and Kaufman, 1985)

Door (Buck, 1948; Burns, 1987; Hammer, 1954, 1958; Jolles, 1971; Kaufman and Wohl, 1992; Oster and Gould, 1987; Van Hutton, 1994; Wohl and Kaufman, 1985)

Fence (Van Hutton, 1994)

Gutters (Oster and Gould, 1987)

Roof (Hammer, 1980; Jolles, 1971; Kaufman and Wohl, 1992; Wohl and Kaufman, 1985)

Shutters (Oster and Gould, 1987)

Walkway (Jolles, 1971; Kaufman and Wohl, 1992; Oster and Gould, 1987)

Walls (Jolles, 1971; Kaufman and Wohl, 1992; Oster and Gould, 1987; Wohl and Kaufman, 1985)

Window(s) (Buck, 1966; Burns, 1987; Hammer, 1958, 1980; Jolles, 1971; Kaufman and Wohl, 1992; Oster and Gould, 1987; Van Hutton, 1994; Wohl and Kaufman, 1985)

Tree

Tree (Whole) (Cohen and Cox, 1989; Hammer, 1980; Kaufman and Wohl, 1992; Oster and Gould, 1987; Wohl and Kaufman, 1985)

Type of Tree (Bolander, 1977; Jolles, 1971; Ogdon, 1977; Oster and Gould, 1987; Van Hutton, 1994; Wohl and Kaufman, 1985)

Placement (Bolander, 1977; Buck, 1973; Di Leo, 1983)

Branches (Buck, 1981; Hammer, 1980; Jolles, 1969, 1971; Kaufman and Wohl, 1992; Koch, 1952; Ogdon, 1977; Van Hutton, 1994; Wohl and Kaufman, 1985)

Crown, Leaves (Di Leo, 1970; Buck, 1981; Kaufman and Wohl, 1992; Oster and Gould, 1987, Van Hutton, 1994; Wohl and Kaufman, 1985)

Trunk (Bolander, 1977; Buck, 1981; Di Leo, 1970, 1983; Hammer, 1980; Kaufman and Wohl, 1992; Lyons, 1955; Oster and Gould, 1987; Van Hutton, 1994; Wohl and Kaufman, 1985)

Roots (Buck, 1973; Di Leo, 1970; Hammer, 1980; Jolles, 1971; Kaufman and Wohl, 1992; Oster and Gould, 1987; Wohl and Kaufman, 1985)

Knotholes (Di Leo, 1983; Hammer, 1980; Kaufman and Wohl, 1992; Oster and Gould, 1987; Wohl and Kaufman, 1985)

Frequently Drawn Miscellaneous Details

(Buck, 1948, 1966; Burns, 1987; Culbertson and Revel, 1987; Di Leo, 1983; Hammer, 1954, 1958; Jolles, 1971; Kaufman and Wohl, 1992; Kelley, 1984; Machover, 1949, 1980; Malchiodi, 1990; Ogdon, 1977; Oster and Gould, 1987; Van Hutton, 1994; Wohl and Kaufman, 1985)

acting in A withdrawal or passive behavior that brings about temporary partial relief of inner tension. It is the opposite of acting out behavior although the causes are the same.

acting out An action rather than a verbal response to an unconscious instinctual drive or impulse that brings about temporary partial relief of inner tension. Relief is attained by reacting to a present situation as if it were the situation that originally gave rise to the drive or impulse. (*Modern Synopsis of Psychiatry*, 1972)

conduct disorder A repetitive and persistent pattern of behavior in which the basic rights of others or major age–appropriate societal norms or rules are violated. The behaviors fall into four groups: aggressive, nonaggressive, deceitfulness or theft, and serious violations of rules. (*DSM-IV*)

depersonalization Characterized by a feeling of detachment or estrangement from one's self. The individual may feel like an automaton; living in a dream; being an outside observer of one's mental process, body, or parts of the body. (*DSM-IV*)

ego Ego represents that part of the personality that serves as an honest broker between the id, the superego, and the external world. It controls motility and seeks to achieve a reasonable compromise between the needs of the id and superego. *Encyclopedia of Psychoanalysis*)

family of origin Original nuclear family.

intact family Family with mother, father, and children in one home.

obsessive compulsive disorder Preoccupation with orderliness, perfectionism, and mental and interpersonal control at the expense of flexibility, openness, and efficiency. Attempts to maintain a sense of control through painstaking attention to rules, trivial details, procedures, lists, schedules; being excessively careful and prone to repetition. (*DSM-IV*)

pathology Any deviation from a healthy, normal, or efficient condition. (*Webster's Unabridged Dictionary*)

projection A defense mechanism employed by the unconscious through which internal impulses and feelings that are unacceptable to the total personality are attributed to an external object. (*Encyclopedia of Psychoanalysis*)

regression Unconscious defense mechanism in which a person undergoes a partial or total return to earlier patterns of adaptation.

superego Denotative of that part of the total personality that consists of the ego-ideal and the conscience. Inhibitory forces from the outer world have been internalized. It is the driver that pushes us to strive toward the ideal goal. (*Encyclopedia of Psychoanalysis*)

transparencies An X–Ray-like ability to see through solid objects, e.g. , a drawing of an exterior view of the house with the artist drawing objects inside the house, giving the viewer the impression of seeing through the walls.

BIBLIOGRAPHY

Blain, G., Bergner, R., Lewis, M., & Goldstein, M. "The Use of Objectively Scorable House-Tree-Person Indicators to Establish Child Abuse." *Journal of Clinical Psychology,* 37(3): 667–673, (1981).

Bolander, K. *Assessing Personality through Tree Drawings.* New York: Basic Books, 1977.

Browne, A. & Finkelhor, D. "Impact of Child Sexual Abuse; A Review of the Research." *Psychological Bulletin,* 99 (1): 66–77, (1987).

Buck, J. N. "The H-P-T Technique: A Qualitative and Quantitative Scoring Manual." *Journal of Clinical Psychology,* 4: 317–396, (1948).

Buck, J. N. *The House-Tree-Person Technique: Revised Manual.* Los Angeles: Western Psychological Services, 1966.

Buck, J. N. *The House-Tree-Person Technique: Revised Manual.* Los Angeles: Western Psychological Services, 1973.

Buck, J. N. *The House-Tree-Person Technique: Revised Manual.* Los Angeles: Western Psychological Services, 1981.

Buck, J. N.: *The House-Tree-Person Technique, Revised Manual.* Los Angeles: Western Psychological Services, 1985.

Buck, J. N. and Hammer, E. F. (Eds.) *Advances in House-Tree-Person Techniques: Variations and Applications.* Los Angeles: Western Psychological Services, 1969.

Burgess, A., McCausland, M. & Wolvert, W. "Children's Drawings as Indicators of Sexual Trauma." *Perspectives in Psychiatric Care,* 19 (2): 50–58, (1981).

Burns, R. C. *Self-Growth in Families, Kinetic Family Drawings, Research and Application.* New York: Brunner/Mazel, 1982.

Burns, R. C. *Kinetic House-Tree-Person Drawings: An Interpretative Manual.* New York: Brunner/Mazel, 1987.

Burns, R. C. & Kaufman, S. M. *Kinetic Family Drawings (K-F-F): An Introduction to Understanding Children through Kinetic Drawings.* New York: Brunner/Mazel, 1970.

Burns, R. C. & Kaufman, S. M. *Actions, Styles and Symbols in Kinetic Family Drawing, An Interpretative Manual.* New York: Brunner/Mazel, 1972.

Clark, R. E. & Clark, J. *The Encyclopedia of Child Abuse.* New York: Facts on File, 1989.

Cohen, B. & Cox, C. "Breaking the Code: Identification of Multiplicity through Art Productions." *Dissociation,* 1(3): 132–137, (1989).

Cohen, F. & Phelps, R. "Incest Markers in Children's Artwork." *The Arts in Psychotherapy,* 12: 165-383, (1985).

Culbertson, F. & Revel, A. "Graphic Characteristics on the Draw-a-Person Test for Identification of Physical Abuse." *Art Therapy Journal,* July 1987.

Demause, L. "The Universality of Incest." *Journal of Psychohistory,* 18 (1): 1–29, Summer 1990.

Demause, L. "The Sexual Abuse of Children." *Journal of Psychohistory,* 19(2): 123–164, Fall 1991.

Diagnostic and Statistical Manual of Mental Disorders. Fourth Edition. Washington, D.C.: American Psychiatric Association, 1994.

Di Leo, J. H. *Young Children and Their Drawings.* New York: Brunner/Mazel, 1970.

Di Leo, J. H. *Children's Drawings as Diagnostic Aids.* New York: Brunner/Mazel, 1973.

Di Leo, J. H. *Interpreting Children's Drawings.* New York: Brunner/Mazel, 1983.

Eidelberg, L. *Encyclopedia of Psychoanalysis.* New York: The Free Press, 1968.

Findelhor, D. and Browne, A. "The Traumatic Impact of Child Sexual Abuse: A Conceptualization, *American Journal of Orthopsychiatry,* 55(4): 530–541, (1985).

Hammer, E. F. "A Comparison of HTP's of Rapists and Pedophiles." *Journal of Projective Techniques,* 18: 346–354, (1954).

Hammer, E. F. *The Clinical Application of Projective Drawings.* Springfield, IL: Charles C. Thomas, 1958.

Hammer, E. F. *The Clinical Application of Projective Drawings.* Springfield, IL; Charles C. Thomas, 1980.

Hammer, E. F. "The Use of the H-T-P in Criminal Court: Acting out." In J. N. Buck and E. F. Hammer (Eds.) *Advances in House-Tree-Person Techniques: Variations and Applications* (pp. 267–295). Los Angeles: Western Psychological Services, 1969.

Handler, L. & Reyher, J. "The Effects of Stress on the Draw-a-Person Test." *Journal of Counseling Psychology.* 259–264, (1964).

Hibbard, R., Roughmann, K., & Hoekelman, R. "Genitalia in Children's Drawings: An Association with Sexual Abuse." *Pediatrics* 79(1): 129–137, (1987).

Jolles, I. A. "The Use of the H-T-P in a School Setting." In J. N. Buck & E. F. Hammer (Eds.) *Advances in House-Tree-Person Techniques: Variations and Applications* (pp. 223–243). Los Angeles: Western Psychological Services, 1969.

Jolles, I. A. *A Catalogue for the Qualitative Interpretation of the H-T-P.* Los Angeles: Western Psychological Services, 1971.

Kaufman, B. & Wohl, A. *Casualties of Childhood, A Developmental Perspective on Sexual Abuse Using Projective Drawings.* New York: Brunner/Mazel, 1992.

Kelley, S. "The Use of Art Therapy with the Sexually Abused Child." *Journal of Psychosocial Nursing and Mental Health Services,* 22(12): 12–18, (1984).

Kelley, S. "Children's Drawings as Indicators of Sexual Trauma." *Perspectus in Psychiatric Care,* 11 (2): 50–58, (1984).

Kelley, S. "Drawings: Critical Communications for Sexually Abused Children." *Pediatric Nursing,* 11: 421–426, (1985).

Kellogg, R. *Analyzing Children's Art.* Palo Alto, CA: Mayfield Publishing, 1970.

Klepsch, M. & Logie, L. *Children Draw and Tell.* New York: Brunner/Mazel, 1982.

Koch, C. *The Tree Test.* New York: Grune & Stratton, 1952.

Koppitz, E. M. *Psychological Evaluation of Children's Human Figure Drawings.* New York: Grune & Stratton, 1968.

Landgarten, H. B. *Clinical Art Therapy, A Comprehensive Guide.* New York: Brunner/Mazel, 1981.

Levick, M. *Mommy, Daddy, Look What I'm Saying, What Children Are Telling You through Their Art.* New York: M. Evans & Co., 1986.

Lyons, J. "The Scar on the H-T-P Tree." *Journal of Clinical Psychology,* 11: 267–270, (1955).

Machover, K. *Personality Projection in the Drawings of the Human Figure.* Springfield, IL: Charles C. Thomas, 1949.

Machover, K. *Personality Projection in the Drawing of the Human Figure.* Springfield, IL: Charles C. Thomas, 1980.

Malchiodi, C. *Breaking the Silence, Art Therapy with Children from Violent Homes.* New York: Brunner/ Mazel, 1990.

Ogdon, D. *Psychodiagnostics and Personality Assessment: A Handbook.* Los Angeles: Western Psychological Services, 1977.

Oster, G. D. & Gould, P. *Using Drawings in Assessment and Therapy. A Guide For Mental Health Professionals.* New York: Brunner/Mazel, 1987.

Saarni, C. & Azara, V. "Developmental Analyses of Human Figure Drawings in Adolescence, Young Adulthood, and Middle Age." *Journal of Personality Assessment,* 41: 31–38, (1977).

Shneidman, E. S. "Some Relationships between Thematic and Drawing Materials." In E. F. Hammer (Ed.), *The Clinical Application of Projective Drawings* (pp. 620–627). Springfield, IL: Charles C. Thomas, 1958.

Stember, C. "Existential Art Therapy," *Rape, Crisis and Recovery.* A. Burgess & L. Holmstrom (Eds.), Bowie, MD: Brady Co., 1978.

Tufts' New England Medical Center, Division of Child Psychiatry. *Sexually Exploited Children; Service and Research Project*. Final report for the Office of Juvenile Justice and Delinquency Prevention. Washington, DC: U.S. Department of Justice, 1984.

Van Hutton, V. *House-Tree-Person and Draw-a-Person as Measures of Abuse in Children: A Quantitative Scoring System*. Odessa, FL: Psychological Assessment Resources, Inc., 1994.

Wissow, L. S. "Child Abuse and Neglect," *New England Journal of Medicine*, 332(21): 1425–1431, (1995).

Wohl, A. & Kaufman, B. *Silent Screams and Hidden Cries. An Interpretation of Artwork by Children from Violent Homes*. New York: Brunner/Mazel, 1985.

I N D E X

HOLLY PRESS

To Order. . .

• FAX (805) 563-9923

• Voice Mail (805) 563-9923 *Have your VISA or MasterCard ready*

• Mail *Complete order form below*

YES, I want to order by mail *Detecting Child Abuse: Recognizing Children at Risk through Drawings.*

QUANTITY_____ x $19.95   _____

SALES TAX (add 7.75% sales tax in CA)   _____

SHIPPING & HANDLING   _____
Book rate add $2.00 for the first book
and 75 cents each additional book.
(Surface shipping three to four weeks)

AIR MAIL $3.50 per book.   _____

TOTAL   _____

SHIP TO:

Institution _____

Name _____

Address _____

City _____ State _____ Zip _____

Telephone: (   ) _____

BILL TO: (attach if different from SHIP TO)

PAYMENT
❑ Check (payable to Holly Press)
❑ VISA ❑ MasterCard

Card Number _____ Exp. Date _____

Signature _____ Date _____

GUARANTEE
I understand that I may return the book/s for a full refund — for any reason, no questions asked.

MAIL TO:
Holly Press
P.O. Box 24136-121
Santa Barbara, CA 93121